P9-CEC-272

# U.S. History I

*by*
*Paul Soifer, Ph.D.*
*Abraham Hoffman, Ph.D.*

Wiley Publishing, Inc.

CliffsQuickReview™ *U.S. History I*

Published by:
Wiley Publishing, Inc.
111 River Street
Hoboken, NJ 07030-5774
www.wiley.com

Copyright © 1998 Wiley Publishing, Inc., New York, New York
ISBN: 978-0-8220-5360-6
Printed in the United States of America
15 14 13 12 11
1O/TR/QT/QY/IN
Published by Wiley Publishing, Inc., New York, NY
Published simultaneously in Canada

For general information on our other products and services or to obtain technical support, please contact our Customer Care Department within the U.S. at 800-762-2974, outside the U.S. at 317-572-3993, or fax 317-572-4002.

Wiley also publishes its books in a variety of electronic formats. Some content that appears in print may not be available in electronic books.

This book provides the student with an overview of United States history from before the colonial period through the end of Reconstruction. Students will find this book helpful as a supplement to major textbooks in the field or as a summary of the major issues and events in U.S. history. We hope students will make effective use of this book, and we welcome any questions they may direct to us at Cliffs Notes.

We would like to express our deep appreciation to Linnea Fredrickson, our editor, for her patience, valuable suggestions on organization, and useful questions on the text, which helped us improve the narrative.

*The Authors*

# CONTENTS

# CONTENTS

# CONTENTS

# CONTENTS

# CONTENTS

# CONTENTS

# CONTENTS

# CONTENTS

## The First Inhabitants of the Western Hemisphere

In telling the history of the United States and also of the nations of the Western Hemisphere in general, historians have wrestled with the problem of what to call the hemisphere's first inhabitants. Under the mistaken impression he had reached the "Indies," explorer Christopher Columbus called the people he met "Indians." This was an error in identification that has persisted for more than five hundred years, for the inhabitants of North and South America had no collective name by which they called themselves.

Historians, anthropologists, and political activists have offered various names, none fully satisfactory. Anthropologists have used "aborigine," but the term suggests a primitive level of existence inconsistent with the cultural level of many tribes. Another term, "Amerindian," which combines Columbus's error with the name of another Italian explorer, Amerigo Vespucci (whose name was the source of "America"), lacks any historical context. Since the 1960s, "Native American" has come into popular favor, though some activists prefer "American Indian." In the absence of a truly representative term, descriptive references such as "native peoples" or "indigenous peoples," though vague, avoid European influence. In recent years, some argument has developed over whether to refer to tribes in the singular or plural—Apache or Apaches—with supporters on both sides demanding political correctness.

**Arrival of the first inhabitants.** Apart from the brief visit of the Scandinavians in the early eleventh century, the Western Hemisphere remained unknown to Europe until Columbus's voyage in 1492. However, the native peoples of North and South America arrived from Asia long before, in a series of migrations that began perhaps as early as forty thousand years ago across the land bridge that connected Siberia and Alaska.

The first Americans found a hunter's paradise. Mammoths and mastodons, ancestors of the elephant, and elk, moose, and caribou abounded on the North American continent. Millions of bison lived on the Great Plains, as did antelope, deer, and other game animals, providing the earliest inhabitants of the Americas, the **Paleo-Indians,** with a land rich in food sources. Because food was abundant, the population grew, and human settlement spread throughout the Western Hemisphere rather quickly.

The Paleo-Indians were hunter-gatherers who lived in small groups of not more than fifty people. They were constantly on the move, following the herds of big game, apparently recognizing the rights of other bands to hunting grounds. These early native people developed a fluted stone point for spears that made their hunting more efficient. Evidence of such fluted points has surfaced throughout the Americas.

**Life on the North American continent.** Anthropologists have found an astonishing variety of culture and language groups among the native peoples of North America. Tribes living in close proximity might have spoken totally unrelated languages, while tribes living hundreds of miles from each other might have shared similar languages. Regions in which a population shares a similar lifestyle based on environmental conditions are known as **culture areas.** Although North America can be divided into many such regions, the most significant are the Southwest, Great Plains, and Eastern Woodlands.

**The Southwest.** Following the climate changes after the end of the last ice age (about ten thousand years ago), agriculture gradually developed in North America. The native peoples of central Mexico began planting maize, beans, and squash around 5000 B.C., and the cultivation of these crops slowly spread northward. In the desert Southwest, the **Hohokam** culture (southern Arizona) constructed an elaborate network of irrigation canals to water their fields. Farming meant a settled life, and the Hohokam lived in permanent villages with as many as several hundred residents. The villages served as economic, religious, and political centers.

East of the Hohokam, the **Anasazi** lived where the states of New Mexico, Arizona, Colorado, and Utah meet at the Four Corners. The Anasazi built permanent homes and developed villages with as many as fifteen hundred people. At the high point of Anasazi culture, Chaco Canyon in northwestern New Mexico had twelve villages sustaining some fifteen thousand people, with straight roads connecting outlying settlements. Both the Hohokam and Anasazi established trade connections with tribes in what would become Mexico and California.

A major and dramatic change affected the Hohokam and Anasazi societies in the twelfth and thirteenth centuries, however. At that time, a prolonged drought drastically reduced the water supply in the region. The area could no longer provide for a large population, and the villages were abandoned as the people left in search of more hospitable areas, many settling along the upper Rio Grande and establishing the pueblos that continue to this day.

**The Great Plains.** In contrast to the Southwest tribes, early native peoples of the Great Plains were hunters, relying on bison and other Plains animals to provide food, clothing, and shelter. Tribes followed the large bison herds and claimed extensive areas as their hunting grounds. Conflicts over territory led to a perpetual rivalry among the tribes that bordered on warfare.

With their dependence on hunting, Plains tribes had difficulty maintaining their standard of living. Of necessity nomadic, they were compelled to keep material possessions to a minimum. Their only domesticated animal was the dog. Limited to what they could carry with them, Plains peoples lived a harsh existence. The horse, introduced with the arrival of the Europeans in the sixteenth century, transformed the culture of the Great Plains.

**The Eastern Woodlands.** The "Eastern Woodlands" refers to the large, heavily forested area extending from the Mississippi River to the Atlantic seacoast, where several important cultures flourished. The **Adena** of the Ohio River Valley (fifth century B.C.), who left hundreds of burial mounds, developed into a larger cultural group known as the **Hopewell,** which continued to build elaborate earthen works. Although the Adena-Hopewell peoples remained primarily hunter-gatherers, archeological evidence indicates that they had an extensive trading network stretching to the Rocky Mountains and the Gulf and Atlantic coasts.

The first true farmers of the Eastern Woodlands were the **Mississippians** of the central Mississippi River Valley. The most important Mississippian center was Cahokia, which was located near the confluence of the Missouri and Mississippi Rivers (St. Louis, Missouri). Cahokia had as many as forty thousand residents in a six-square-mile area, and by the thirteenth century its large population was straining to grow enough food to sustain itself. Aggressive neighbors also contributed to the instability of Cahokia, and the people finally scattered to form smaller villages.

**Early North American society and culture.** Estimates of the population of North America at the time of European contact have been revised upward by modern scholarship to as many as ten million. Although the native peoples varied widely, they did share some important social and cultural traits.

In modern America, society is chiefly based on the nuclear family (mother, father, and children), but **kinship groups**—the extended family of aunts, uncles, and cousins—were key to the social relations among the native peoples. Among tribes as different as the Pueblo of the Southwest and the Iroquois of the Northeast, kinship was determined by the female line. The **clan** was composed of several kinship groups that claimed descent from a common ancestor, often a woman. The roles assigned to men and women were clearly defined. The men hunted, engaged in trade, made war, and were the tribal leaders, while the women cared for the children, gathered food, and cultivated crops. The exception to this pattern was in the Southwest where men also worked the fields. In societies where matrilineal descent was important, women had more responsibilities. They controlled property, distributed food, and either advised or were the real power in tribal councils.

Native peoples believed that nature was sacred. The sun, moon, stars, mountains, rivers, trees, and animals had spiritual power and were either the gods themselves or the abode of gods. Tribal creation myths were most often based on the interplay of these natural forces. While some tribes accepted the idea of a supreme being, polytheism was the rule. The **shaman** was considered the intermediary between the people and the gods in the spirit world. He or she also interpreted the visions and dreams that were an important part of religious practice. To induce dreams, an individual might fast for several days, use drugs, or go through a physical ordeal. In addition to rituals to bring rain or ensure a good harvest or hunt, ceremonies marking life-cycle events—birth, puberty, marriage, and death—were common.

There is a tendency to view North American society at the end of the fifteenth century as a pre-Columbian Garden of Eden corrupted by the arrival of the Europeans. This notion of an idyllic place where everyone was one with the environment and each other denies native peoples their own history. The Mississippians, for example, practiced torture and human sacrifice as part of their death cult. Tribes in the Pacific Northwest had a very rigid class structure based on private property and made slaves out of war captives and debtors. Among the Natchez in the Southeast, the hereditary nobles under the chief, or "Great Sun," oppressed the majority of the tribe.

## European Contact

For the native peoples of North America, contact with Europeans was less dramatic than that experienced by the Aztec and Inca empires upon the arrival of the Spanish *conquistadors*. Nonetheless, Spanish explorers attempting to penetrate into what would become the United States left three major legacies for the tribes: disease, horses and other domesticated animals, and metal tools and firearms.

**Disease.** The most serious threat the native peoples faced was not the superior arms of the Europeans but the diseases they brought with them to the New World. With the possible exception of syphilis, the Western Hemisphere was effectively free of infectious disease prior to European contact. The indigenous population, with no reservoir of natural immunity or built-up resistance, succumbed quickly to diphtheria, mumps, measles, and smallpox. Smallpox, the main killer, spread rapidly beyond the initial European carriers. Tribes that met and traded over long distances infected one another and carried the disease back to their villages. There is evidence that smallpox had already surfaced in Peru sometime before the arrival of Francisco Pizarro in 1532.

Estimates of the depopulation of the native peoples of North America as a result of disease run as high as ninety percent in many regions, and, in some instances, even the knowledge of the existence of certain tribes was obliterated. Infection carried by Spanish explorers traveling along the Gulf Coast annihilated the tribes of the lower Mississippi River so that their cultural presence, visible in the form of their burial mounds, was largely unrecognized until the twentieth century. The devastating impact of disease was not limited to just the years of initial contact. In 1804, Meriwether Lewis and William Clark, leaders of the Corps of Discovery, were given hospitality by the Mandans during their winter stay at Fort Mandan on the Missouri River. The tribe, which numbered about 2000, dwindled to 150 after an epidemic of smallpox brought by fur traders in 1837.

**Horses and other domesticated animals.** Although disease proved a curse to the native peoples, the introduction of European livestock improved the quality of life for many tribes. The best known and most dramatic change came with the horse, but other domesticated animals were important as well. Cattle, sheep, goats, and hogs were raised for food, and their hides were used for clothing, blankets, and shelter coverings.

The arrival of the horse in North America, which probably occurred with the 1540 expedition of Francisco Vásquez de Coronado into the Southwest, transformed Plains Indian culture. By the end of the sixteenth century, horses were being traded, stolen, or left to stray, and their numbers multiplied. The Sioux, Cheyenne, and Kiowa soon found the horse indispensable, and its use spread to other tribes. A simple tied arrangement of poles made from young trees enabled horses to pull large loads. The poles doubled as a *tipi* framework and enabled the dwellings of these nomadic peoples to be larger and more comfortable. Mounted on horseback, the Indians became dramatically more efficient hunters of bison. Within a generation, the Plains Indians made the horse an integral part of their culture. Frontiersmen crossing the Mississippi and encountering Indians on horseback in the eighteenth century had no idea that the horse culture was less than two hundred years old.

The introduction of a variety of domesticated animals came with a price tag apparent to neither the native peoples nor the Europeans for some time. European settlers fed livestock with European grains. These grains, including wheat, oats, rye, and a wide range of other grasses, took to North American soil in much the same way that crabgrass and weeds attack a carefully tended lawn. Slowly, the landscape of North America changed as native grasses gave way to foreign varieties. Not until late in the twentieth century would the environmental changes be fully noticed or even start to be assessed.

**Metal tools and firearms.** Technologically, native peoples were in the Stone Age. As finely wrought and useful as their basketry, pottery, and obsidian blades may have been, Native Americans lacked the knowledge to make metal tools. The knives, needles, fishhooks, hatchets, and pots offered by the Europeans were immediately recognized as more efficient than their stone, bone, or clay implements.

Early firearms—muskets and pistols—did not present a clear advantage for the Europeans over the Indians. The guns were not especially accurate over more than a short distance, took time to reload, and were difficult to repair; Native Americans initially found their own bows and arrows still quite effective against them. Even the Puritans recognized the limitations of their firearms when they passed a law in 1645 calling for militia training in pikes and bows and arrows as well as muskets.

The balance of firepower changed though by the late eighteenth century as muskets evolved into rifles with much greater accuracy. By the end of the Civil War, repeating rifles and six-shot revolvers put the bow and arrow at a severe disadvantage. Native Americans did not reject the rifle, and many learned to pour lead into molds for bullets. Improvements in weapons technology, however, left them dependent on whites for firearms and ammunition as well as most metal goods. The Native Americans could not replicate the complex mechanisms of a Winchester or Colt, and cartridges requiring a molded bullet, shell casing, and gunpowder were beyond their ability to duplicate. By the end of the nineteenth century, Euroamerican technology had overwhelmed the Native Americans.

**The great biological exchange.** European contact did not affect only the native peoples; there was a genuine, if perhaps unequal, exchange. Many new crop and food plants, such as maize, beans, potatoes, peanuts, pumpkins, and avocados, were first introduced to Europe from the Western Hemisphere. **Maize,** or Indian corn, was perhaps the most important of them. Capable of growing in almost any climate or soil, it soon became a staple around the world.

The old view that Columbus "discovered" America has been replaced by the idea that he "encountered" America. The rephrasing recognizes that there were already millions of people in the Western Hemisphere in 1492 with their distinct and developed cultures who merit being acknowledged as the first Americans. There is no doubt that contact with Europeans was devastating to the native population both then and later. While the conquest was certainly inevitable, oversimplification should be avoided. It did not take place all at once in all places. Confrontation was sudden and subjugation immediate in some locales, while in others the native peoples remained unaware of the Europeans' presence for centuries. California Indians knew almost nothing of the Europeans until 1769, and the Shawnee still looked to a British alliance to keep American settlers south of the Ohio River as late as 1812.

At the end of the fifteenth century, the confluence of a number of long-developing factors and several major events launched the European exploration and colonization of the Western Hemisphere. In 1096, European Christians had embarked on a succession of military expeditions to free Palestine from Muslim rule. Although ultimately unsuccessful, these **Crusades** fostered economic ties between Europe and the Middle and Far East. Trade in spices (which were needed to preserve food) and silks attracted the new merchant class that was emerging in the growing medieval cities. The Italian Marco Polo's account of his travels to and extended stay in China at the end of the thirteenth century further stimulated interest in Asia, and the city-states of Genoa and Venice became the centers of international trade.

As Europe slowly recovered from the devastating effects of the **Black Death** (1347–51), the epidemic of bubonic plague that killed a third of its population, political developments disrupted economic ties with Asia. In 1453, the Muslim Ottoman Turks captured Constantinople, strategically located on the eastern Mediterranean. As Ottoman power spread throughout the Middle East, Europeans found their traditional overland trade routes effectively blocked. The prohibitively high tribute charged by the Turks led to dramatic price increases for luxury products from the Far East. Searching for a solution to this dilemma, European merchants reasoned that if land routes were problematical, perhaps trade could continue by sea.

## The Portuguese Explorations and West Africa

Motivated by the desire for new markets and an ongoing opposition to the Muslims, Portuguese sailors had begun to explore the West African coast in the first half of the fifteenth century. The expeditions were sponsored by Prince Henry of Portugal, who founded a center for seamanship around 1420 and earned himself the title of the Navigator. At the center, information about tides and currents was collected, more accurate charts and maps were drawn, techniques for determining longitude were improved, and new ship designs (such as the caravel) were developed. With these innovations, the Portuguese reached the westernmost point of the continent at Cape Verde in 1448, setting up a lucrative network of trading posts along the way. The most significant voyages, however, came forty years later. Bartolomeu Dias rounded the Cape of Good Hope at the southern tip of Africa in 1488. A decade later, Vasco da Gama sailed around Africa and reached the Malabar Coast of India, establishing an all-water route to Asia. Over the next twenty years, Portugal made Goa its major trading center in India, established outposts in Malaysia, and set up direct contact with China. The Muslim monopoly on the spice trade in Asia was broken.

**The West African kingdoms.** One consequence of the Portuguese expeditions was contact with West Africa. The sub-Saharan kingdoms—Ghana, Mali, Benin, Songhai, and Kongo—were well-organized societies with a long history, but they were almost unknown to Europeans. Until the Muslim invasions of the eleventh century, the Ghana empire had extensive commercial ties with North Africa, Egypt, and the Middle East. Mali, an Islamic state whose capital Timbuktu was a major economic and cultural center, controlled the gold trade. The arrival of the Portuguese brought about a dramatic shift in the flow of African gold. Rather than going overland by caravan to North Africa and then into the coffers of the commercially powerful Italian city-states, the precious metal was shipped by sea directly to Lisbon and western Europe.

The Portuguese were interested in slaves as well as gold. Arab merchants had bought slaves in West Africa as early as the eighth century, and they continued to act as middlemen when the Europeans arrived. Portugal used African slaves as early as 1497 in the sugarcane fields on the islands it took over off the African coast. Millions of blacks were shipped from West African ports to work plantations in North and South America over the next three hundred years. Slavery in the New World, justified on economic and racial grounds, was quite different from that in Africa. Although slavery was an accepted social institution throughout the continent, the slaves were typically prisoners of war, debtors, or criminals, and their condition was neither permanent nor hereditary.

## Christopher Columbus and the Spanish Explorations

Christopher Columbus, a Genoese sailor, believed that sailing west across the Atlantic Ocean was the shortest sea route to Asia. Ignorant of the fact that the Western Hemisphere lay between Europe and Asia and assuming the earth's circumference to be a third less than it actually is, he was convinced that Japan would appear on the horizon just three thousand miles to the west. Like other seafarers of his day, Columbus was untroubled by political allegiances; he was ready to sail for whatever country would pay for his voyage. Either because of his arrogance (he wanted ships and crews to be provided at no expense to himself) or ambition (he insisted on governing the lands he discovered), he found it difficult to find a patron. The Portuguese rejected his plan twice, and the rulers of England and France were not interested. With influential supporters at court, Columbus convinced King Ferdinand and Queen Isabella of Spain to partially underwrite his expedition. In 1492, Granada, the last Muslim stronghold on the Iberian Peninsula, had fallen to the forces of the Spanish monarchs. With the *Reconquista* complete and Spain a unified country, Ferdinand and Isabella could turn their attention to overseas exploration.

**The voyages of Columbus.** Columbus set sail with three small ships and a crew of eighty-seven men on August 2, 1492, and made landfall on October 12 on an island in the Bahamas that he called San Salvador. Over the next several months, he explored the island that is now Cuba and another island he named Hispaniola (Santo Domingo), where he came across the first significant amount of gold. Ferdinand and Isabella financed a much larger expedition with seventeen ships and more than twelve hundred men soon after his return to Spain. During his second voyage, Columbus explored the islands that are now called Puerto Rico and Jamaica and established the first permanent Spanish settlement on Hispaniola. He made two additional voyages: between 1498 and 1500 to the Caribbean and the northern coast of South America, and between 1502 and 1504 to the coast of Central America.

Columbus's success created the potential for conflict between Spain and Portugal. Ferdinand and Isabella were anxious to protect their claims to the new lands. In May 1493, very soon after Columbus returned from his first voyage, they persuaded Pope Alexander VI to issue an edict giving Spain all lands west of an imaginary line through the Atlantic. Portugal was not satisfied. Through the **Treaty of Tordesillas** (1494), the two countries agreed to move the line further west and give Portugal exclusive right to the territory to the east. Although the result of the shift was unknown at the time, the change put the eastern quarter of South America (Brazil) in the Portuguese sphere; Pedro Cabral reached the Brazilian coast in 1500.

Columbus referred to the lands he discovered as "the Indies" and the people he encountered as "Indians" (*Indios,* in Spanish). He never wavered from the belief that he had reached the outlying islands off the Asian mainland. Amerigo Vespucci, another Italian navigator, sailed extensively along the coast of South America as a member of both Spanish and Portuguese expeditions and is considered to be the first to realize that the Indies were in fact a "New World" and not part of Asia. The first map that identified known parts of the Western Hemisphere as "America," after Vespucci, was published in 1507.

**The Spanish conquests of Central and South America.** In the half century after Columbus's death, Spain established an extensive empire in the Western Hemisphere that stretched from the region of Mexico to the tip of South America and out into the Pacific Ocean. Ferdinand Magellan's voyage around the world (1519–22), in addition to demonstrating the true circumference of the earth, was the basis for a Spanish colony in the Philippines. In the same year Magellan set sail, Hernan Cortés and about six hundred men landed on the Gulf

Coast of Mexico and marched inland to Tenochtitlán (modern Mexico City), the capital of the Aztec empire. He was able to take advantage of the Aztec belief that the Europeans might be returning gods, make strategic alliances with disaffected local tribes, and use his horses and superior firepower to capture the city in 1521. The Spaniards conquered the other native cultures in Central and South America in quick succession. The Toltec-Mayans of the Yucatan Peninsula and Guatemala fell between 1522 and 1528. Francisco Pizarro, benefiting from internal strife in the Inca empire, took Peru (1531–33) with an army that numbered less than two hundred. From there, Spanish forces moved south down the west side of the continent and east into what would become Columbia.

The early Spanish explorer-adventurers, the *conquistadors,* were more interested in finding gold and silver than in colonization, and they relied on the native peoples to work the sugarcane fields of the Caribbean and the mines of Mexico and Peru. While the exploitation of the native peoples had its critics, most notably in the Catholic priest Bartolomé de Las Casas, it was disease rather than harsh treatment at the hands of the Spaniards that devastated the indigenous population. First on Hispaniola and then on the mainland, millions died from smallpox, measles, and other infections. African slaves were brought to the West Indies as early as 1503 because of a critical labor shortage.

**Spain in North America.** Stories and legends about incredible wealth stimulated the Spanish exploration of North America. The earliest expedition brought Juan Ponce de León to the Florida peninsula in search of the mythical "Fountain of Youth" (1513). In 1528, Panfilo de Narváez sailed along the Gulf Coast of the United States, but was shipwrecked off what is now Texas. A small group of survivors under Álvaro Núñez Cabeza de Vaca made its way across Texas and the Southwest region to Mexico. Between 1539 and 1543, Hernando de Soto led a large force from western Florida to the Appalachian Mountains and then west across the Mississippi River with the major consequence of spreading smallpox throughout the lower Mississippi Valley. The search for the fabled riches of the "Seven Golden Cities of Cibola," which de Vaca had mentioned in his account, took Francisco Vasquez de Coronado from northern Mexico as far northeast as present-day Kansas between 1541 and 1543; smaller groups from the main expedition discovered the Grand Canyon and the Colorado River. Meanwhile, Juan Rodriguez Cabrillo sailed up the west coast and claimed the California area for Spain. The founding of the two oldest cities in the United States—St. Augustine, Florida, (1565) and Santa Fe, New Mexico (1609)—was the chief result of almost a century of Spanish exploration.

## French and Dutch Explorations

Although French fishermen had caught cod off Newfoundland as early as 1504, fish were not what motivated the voyages sponsored by King Francis I in the sixteenth century. In 1524, Giovanni da Verrazano sailed up the east coast from present-day North Carolina to Nova Scotia looking for a northwesterly passage to Asia. The same objective was behind Jacques Cartier's three voyages (1534–42) that were the basis for future French claims to Canada. He explored the Gulf of St. Lawrence and discovered the St. Lawrence River, on which members of his expedition founded a short-lived settlement near Quebec. Abortive colonies were also established by French Huguenots (Protestants) within the modern-day boundaries of South Carolina (1562–64) and Florida (1564–65).

The Wars of Religion, which pitted Catholic against Protestant, delayed further French exploration until the seventeenth century. Under the leadership of Samuel de Champlain, who made numerous voyages to the eastern Canada region beginning in 1603, the city of Quebec was founded (1608) and alliances were made with the Hurons to develop the fur trade. Indeed, furs rather than settlements were more important to France at the time. The Dutch became one of the great seafaring and commercial nations of Europe in the seventeenth century and were rivals of the Portuguese in the East Indies. The Dutch East India Company financed English sailor Henry Hudson in 1609 for another search for the elusive Northwest Passage. He discovered Delaware Bay and sailed up the river later named for him, establishing Dutch claims for the territory known as New Netherland. Like the French, the Dutch were fur traders, and they established lucrative ties with the local tribes of the Iroquois Confederacy.

## English Exploration and Early Settlements

With the exception of John Cabot's voyage to Newfoundland in 1497, the English showed little interest in the New World until the reign of Elizabeth I. Wary of confronting powerful Spain directly, Elizabeth secretly supported English seamen who raided Spanish settlements in the Western Hemisphere and captured their treasure ships. Men such as John Hawkins and Francis Drake, popularly known as "sea dogs," received titles from the queen, who shared in their booty. More than fifty years after Magellan circumnavigated the globe, Drake duplicated the feat following attacks against Spanish ports on the west coast of South America (1577–80).

**The lost colony of Roanoke.** While English explorers, most notably Martin Frobisher, continued to look for the Northwest Passage, there was interest in colonizing North America. In 1584, Sir Walter Raleigh scouted possible sites for a colony farther to the south. Naming the land Virginia after Elizabeth, the Virgin Queen, he chose Roanoke Island off the coast of present-day North Carolina. The first attempt to settle there (1585–86) was quickly abandoned. A group of 110 men, women, and children sailed for Roanoke in the following year. The colony's leader, John White, returned to England for additional supplies but did not return until 1590 because of the war between England and Spain. He found no trace of the colonists, and the only message left was the cryptic word "Croatoan" carved on a wooden post. It is most likely that the small settlement was overrun by local tribes, but to this day, no one has explained the meaning of "Croatoan" or found definitive evidence of the fate of the Roanoke colony.

The failure of Roanoke was expensive, and, with the war against Spain still raging, Elizabeth made it clear that there was no money for colonization ventures. When peace came in 1604, private funds rather than the royal treasury financed English settlement in North America.

**The joint-stock company and the founding of Jamestown.** In 1606, Elizabeth's successor, James I, issued charters to the Virginia Company of Plymouth and the Virginia Company of London to establish colonies along the Atlantic coast from modern-day North Carolina to Maine. These were **joint-stock companies,** the forerunner of the modern corporation. Individuals bought stock in the companies, which paid for ships and supplies, hoping to realize a profit from their investment.

The Virginia Company of Plymouth founded a colony at Sagadahoc in Maine in 1607, which quickly failed due to hostility from the local tribes, conflicts among the settlers, and inadequate supplies. The same fate almost befell the London Company's effort at Jamestown near Chesapeake Bay in Virginia. Most of the colonists were gentry unaccustomed to manual labor who wanted to spend their time looking for gold and hunting. Only the leadership of John Smith, who forced everyone to work and who negotiated with the Indians, guaranteed Jamestown's initial survival.

Conditions deteriorated after Smith left in 1609, but there were important developments over the next decade. John Rolfe introduced tobacco as a cash crop, and even though James I was an ardent anti-smoking advocate, it quickly became a valuable export for the colony. To attract labor and new capital, the London Company instituted the **headright system** in 1618. Anyone who paid his or her own passage to Jamestown received fifty acres of land plus another fifty acres for each additional individual they might bring. The latter were **indentured servants,** who agreed to work for their sponsor for a fixed term (usually four to seven years) in return for their passage. There were also newcomers to the colony that came in chains. The first ship to bring African slaves to North America landed at Jamestown in 1619.

Even with the headright system and the influx of indentured servants, Jamestown grew slowly. There were only about twelve hundred settlers by 1622. Death from disease and malnutrition took its
toll, the company was in debt to its shareholders, and conflicts with
the Indians became more common as the colony expanded. These
problems led the king to revoke the charter of the London Company;
Virginia became a royal colony under the direct control of the crown
in 1624.

The English colonies along the east coast of North America in the seventeenth and early eighteenth centuries can be categorized in several ways. Religion was the factor behind the founding of Maryland and the New England colonies, particularly Plymouth, Massachusetts Bay, and Rhode Island, while the settlers in Virginia and the other southern colonies were more concerned with growing tobacco. Although all eventually came under direct control of the English kings, Plymouth, Massachusetts Bay, and Virginia began as corporate colonies financed by joint-stock companies. Maryland, New Jersey, Pennsylvania, and the Carolinas were **proprietary** colonies, based on grants of land to individuals or a small group of men by the king. Moreover, colonial boundaries changed; New Hampshire was carved out of land claimed by Massachusetts Bay. New York was originally New Netherland before the English took it over in 1664 and renamed it. Delaware was founded by the Swedes (New Sweden), became a Dutch colony in 1655, and then came under English control in 1664. The English colonies were not confined to the Atlantic coast of North America but were also established in the Caribbean—in the Bahamas, Jamaica, and Barbados—competing there with the Spanish, French, and Dutch.

## New England Colonies

It has long been understood that the prime motive for the founding of the New England colonies was religious freedom. Certainly what those early colonists wanted was the freedom to worship God as they deemed proper, but they did not extend that freedom to everyone. Those who expressed a different approach to religious worship were not welcome. Puritans especially were intolerant toward those who held views other than their own.

Much of the religious disaffection that found its way across the Atlantic Ocean stemmed from disagreements within the Anglican Church, as the Church of England was called. Those who sought to reform Anglican religious practices—to "purify" the church—became known as **Puritans.** They argued that the Church of England was following religious practices that too closely resembled Catholicism both in structure and ceremony. The Anglican clergy was organized along **episcopalian** lines, with a hierarchy of bishops and archbishops. Puritans called for a **congregationalist** structure in which each individual church would be largely self-governing.

**The Plymouth colony.** A more extreme view was held by the **Separatists,** a small group mainly from the English town of Scrooby, who opposed any accommodation with the Anglican Church. Unlike the Puritans, who were also referred to as **Non-Separatists,** the Separatists advocated a complete break with the Church of England. At first, the Separatists left England for the more tolerant atmosphere of the Netherlands, but after a while, their leaders found the Dutch a little too tolerant; their children were adopting Dutch habits and culture. When the opportunity arose to settle on land granted by the Virginia Company of London, the Separatists accepted the offer. In 1620, they set sail for America on the *Mayflower.* As a result of their migrations, the Separatists became known as the **Pilgrims,** people who undertake a religious journey.

Instead of landing on Virginia Company land, however, the Pilgrims found themselves in what is now southern Massachusetts. Because they were outside the jurisdiction of the company and concerned that new Pilgrims among them might cause problems, the leaders signed the **Mayflower Compact,** an agreement establishing a civil government under the sovereignty of King James I and creating the Plymouth Plantation colony.

The Pilgrims endured terrible hardships in their first years at Plymouth, with disease and starvation taking a toll. Relations with the Indians in the area were mixed; despite the charming folktale of the peaceful "first Thanksgiving," the reality is that the Pilgrims used force to control the local tribes. The infant colony grew slowly, raising maize and trading furs with the nearby Dutch as well as with the Indians. Plymouth Plantation was the first permanent settlement in New England, but beyond that distinction, its place in American history is somewhat exaggerated. Before long, the Pilgrims were eclipsed by the far larger and more important immigration of Non-Separatist Puritans, who started the Massachusetts Bay colony.

**The Massachusetts Bay colony.** Harassment by the Church of England, a hostile Charles I, and an economic recession led the Non-Separatist Puritans to decide to settle in North America. Puritan merchants bought the defunct Virginia Company of Plymouth's charter in 1628 and received royal permission to found a colony in the Massachusetts area north of Plymouth Plantation. Between 1630 and 1640, more than twenty thousand Puritan men, women, and children took part in the "Great Migration" to their new home.

The Puritans brought a high level of religious idealism to their first colony, which their leader John Winthrop described as "a city upon a hill"—a model of piety for all. Almost overnight, they founded a half dozen towns, setting up churches on the congregationalist pattern under the Reverend John Cotton. These churches ran their own affairs, taxed the community to finance operations, and hired and fired ministers. Although church attendance was compulsory, not everyone was deemed worthy of membership. The **New England Way** was a rigorous examination of a person's spiritual beliefs to identify "saints," or those qualified to be a church member. This intimidating test ultimately served to limit church membership and forced the next generation to modify procedures. Education was a high priority in Puritan society because literacy was essential to Bible study. Laws were passed calling for the creation of grammar schools to teach reading and writing, and Harvard College was founded in 1636 to train the clergy.

The narrow views of the Puritan leaders regarding religious conformity provoked opposition. Roger Williams argued for the separation of church and state, and the right of privacy in religious belief, and against compulsory church service. Banished from Massachusetts Bay in 1635, he went south to Narragansett Bay and founded the Providence settlement. In 1644, Williams received royal permission to start the colony of Rhode Island, a haven for other religious dissenters.

Anne Hutchinson was another critic of clerical authority. Puritan leaders called her and her supporters **Antinomians**—individuals opposed to the rule of law. As a woman, she was also seen as a challenger to the traditionally male-dominated society. Tried for sedition, Hutchinson was also exiled as a danger to the colony. She lived in Rhode Island for a time and then moved to New Netherland, where she was killed in 1643 during a conflict between settlers and Indians.

The Puritans brought disease as well as their religion to the New World, and the impact on the native population was the same as it had been in the Caribbean, Mexico, and South America a century earlier. As settlements expanded beyond the coastal region, conflicts with the local tribes became common, with equally devastating results. Notably, for the colonists in Massachusetts Bay and New England, disease was less of a problem than it was in the southern colonies. The cold winters limited travel, and the comparatively small farming communities that were established limited the spread of infection. Death rates dwindled, and life expectancy rose. Improved survival combined with the immigration of entire families contributed to the rapid growth of the population.

Massachusetts Bay was a **theocratic** society, or a society in which the lines between church and state were blurred. Church membership, for example, was required for men to vote for elected local officials. The intent of many of the colony's laws was regulation of personal behavior based on Puritan values. Single men and women could not live on their own. Disrespectful servants, errant husbands, and disobedient wives were subject to civil penalties, and rebellious children could even be put to death. The laws also provided a degree of protection for women by punishing abusive men and compelling fathers to support their children.

Puritan efforts to maintain an intensely ideal religious community did not endure past the first generation. Their restrictive membership requirements in place made it difficult for the Puritan churches to maintain themselves. In 1662, the **Half-Way Covenant** was adopted to address the problem. It allowed the church members' baptized children who would not give testimony to achieve sainthood (and thereby church membership) a "half-way" membership in the congregation. This change in the rules meant that the children's children could receive baptism after all. Without sainthood, however, they could neither vote on church matters nor take communion. Change was also imposed from outside. Massachusetts's 1691 royal charter made property ownership rather than church membership the qualification for voting and provided for the toleration of religious dissenters. The New England Way was breaking down, and a consequence was the Salem witchcraft trials of 1692 and 1693.

Belief in witches and demonic possession was common in the seventeenth century, and many people, mainly middle-aged women, were accused of witchcraft throughout New England. What made the events in Salem Village unique was the extent of the hysteria, which led to the imprisonment of more than one hundred men and women and the execution of twenty. Historians attribute the outbreak to several factors—rivalries between families, a clash of values between a small farming community like Salem Village and the more cosmopolitan commercial center of Salem, and the ties between many of the accused with Anglicans, Quakers, and Baptists, whom the Puritans considered heretics.

**Connecticut, New Hampshire, and Maine.** Connecticut was settled by colonists from Plymouth and Massachusetts Bay in the 1630s. Thomas Hooker, a minister from Cambridge who advocated less stringent views on religious conformity than other Puritan clergy, brought part of his congregation to the territory in 1636. New Haven, on the other hand, was founded two years later by Puritans who found even Massachusetts Bay too liberal. Self-rule was established in 1639 through the Fundamental Orders of Connecticut, the first written constitution to create a government, which followed Hooker's approach and gave the right to vote to all freemen and not just church members.

Relations with the Indians were important in Connecticut's early history. The Pequot War (1636–37) largely wiped out the Pequot tribe and cleared away the last obstacle to the expansion of settlements in the Connecticut River Valley. Despite the Fundamental Orders, Connecticut was really without legal status until 1662, when it was chartered as a royal colony.

New Hampshire and Maine were originally proprietorships granted not by the king but the Council of New England. Both colonies strove to maintain their independence but were only partly successful. Massachusetts effectively controlled New Hampshire until 1679, when it became a separate colony under a royal charter; Maine remained part of Massachusetts until 1820.

## The Chesapeake Colonies: Virginia and Maryland

By 1700, the Virginia colonists had made their fortunes through the cultivation of tobacco, setting a pattern that was followed in Maryland and the Carolinas. In political and religious matters, Virginia differed considerably from the New England colonies. The Church of England was the established church in Virginia, which meant taxpayers paid for the support of the church whether or not they were Anglicans. But church membership ultimately mattered little, since a lack of clergymen and few churches kept many Virginians from attending church. Religion thus was of secondary importance in the Virginia colony.

Virginia's colonial government structure resembled that of England's county courts and contrasted with the theocratic government of Massachusetts Bay. A royal governor appointed justices of the peace, who set tax rates and saw to the building and maintenance of public works, such as bridges and roads. In the 1650s, the colonial assembly adopted a bicameral pattern: the House of Burgesses (the elected lower house) and an appointed Governor's Council. The assembly met regularly, not so much for representative government as for the opportunity to raise taxes.

**The founding of Maryland.** Maryland was the first proprietary colony, based on a grant to Cecilius Calvert, Lord Baltimore, who named the land for Queen Henrietta Maria, wife of Charles I. Lord Baltimore planned for Maryland to serve as a haven for English Catholics who suffered political and religious discrimination in England, but few Catholics actually settled in the colony. Protestants were attracted by the inexpensive land that Baltimore offered to help him pay his debts. Baltimore granted his friends the large estates, which resembled medieval manors and paved the way for the plantation system.

At first, relations between Maryland's Catholics and Protestants seemed amicable. For a time they even shared the same chapel. In 1649, under Baltimore's urging, the colonial assembly passed the **Act of Religious Toleration,** the first law in the colonies granting freedom of worship, albeit only for Christians. By 1654, however, with Maryland's Protestants in the majority, the act was repealed. A near civil war broke out and order was not restored until 1658, when Lord Baltimore was returned to power. Religious squabbles continued for years in the Maryland colony.

**Chesapeake society and economy.** Tobacco was the mainstay of the Virginia and Maryland economies. Plantations were established by riverbanks for the good soil and to ensure ease of transportation. Because wealthy planters built their own wharves on the Chesapeake to ship their crop to England, town development was slow. To cultivate tobacco, planters brought in large numbers of English workers, mostly young men who came as indentured servants. More than 110,000 had arrived in the Chesapeake region by 1700. Each indentured servant meant more land for his sponsor under the headright system, which had the effect of squeezing out small-scale farming.

While New England was a land of towns and villages surrounded by small farms, Virginia and Maryland were characterized by large plantations and little urban development. The emphasis on indentured labor meant that relatively few women settled in the Chesapeake colonies. This fact, combined with the high mortality rate from disease—malaria, dysentery, and typhoid—slowed population growth considerably. The one common link between New England and the Chesapeake was the treatment of the Indians.

Fluctuations in Chesapeake tobacco prices caused a prolonged economic depression from 1660 into the early 1700s. Sadly, disillusioned colonists took out their frustrations on the local Indians. In April 1676, Nathaniel Bacon, a relative of Virginia Governor William Berkeley, led three hundred settlers against peaceful local tribes, killing them all. When Bacon's force grew to twelve hundred men, he decided to drive all Indians out of the colony. Fortunately, Governor Berkeley decided that Bacon's actions were excessive and recalled him, but Bacon's army then rebelled against the colonial government and burned Jamestown. Bacon went so far as to promise freedom to servants and slaves of Berkeley's supporters, but he died suddenly, and his movement fell apart. **Bacon's Rebellion** illustrated the tensions between white and Indian, planter and slave, and have and have-not in the colony, tensions made worse by an economic depression that must have seemed without end.

**Indentured servants and slaves.** The Chesapeake region offered little economic opportunity to indentured servants who had completed their term of obligation. Even with the small amount of capital needed for tobacco cultivation, former indentured servants at best became subsistence farmers, a class ripe for such calls to rebellion as those proposed by Nathaniel Bacon. As the number of new indentured laborers declined because of limited chances for advancement and reports of harsh treatment, they were replaced by African slaves.

Early in the seventeenth century, the status of slave and indentured servant was quite similar. After 1660, the Chesapeake colonies enforced laws that defined slavery as a lifelong and inheritable condition based on race. This made slaves profitable because planters could rely not only on their labor but that of their children as well. The slave population, which numbered about four thousand in Virginia and Maryland in 1675, grew significantly to the end of the century.

## The Restoration Colonies

English settlement of North America was seriously curtailed by the conflict between king and Parliament that led to the English Civil War and the rule of Oliver Cromwell (1649–60). Once the monarchy was restored under Charles II, however, colonization resumed. The Restoration Colonies were all proprietorships granted by Charles to men who had helped him reclaim the throne.

**The Carolinas.** The Carolinas (from the Latin version of Charles, *Carolus*), which originally included the land from the southern border of Virginia to Spanish Florida, were given to eight proprietors in 1663. Settlers from Virginia came into the northern part of the territory in the 1650s, bringing with them the tobacco culture. Small-scale farming and the export of lumber and pitch (tar), much in demand by English shipbuilders, were the basis of the economy. North Carolina became a separate colony in 1691. In the south, where the proprietors focused their interest, things took a different turn. Rice became the staple crop by the 1690s. Because its production was extremely labor intensive, African slaves were imported to drain the swamps and work the fields. The reliance on slaves is not surprising. Not only was the supply of indentured servants limited, but many of the early settlers came from the English colonies in the Caribbean, most notably Barbados, where slavery was well established.

Like many Restoration Colonies, South Carolina attracted diverse religious and ethnic groups. In addition to colonists from Barbados, who were mostly Anglicans, there were German Lutherans, Scotch-Irish Presbyterians, Welsh Baptists, and Spanish Jews. This mix did not promote stability. Relations with the Indians often turned violent as whites enslaved native tribes as well as blacks. The inability of the proprietors to maintain order led to South Carolina's becoming a royal colony in 1729.

**From New Netherland to New York.** The Dutch established two trading posts in 1614: one on Manhattan Island and one to the north on the Hudson River at Albany's present location. A decade later, the newly formed Dutch West India Company set up the first permanent settlements, the most important of which was New Amsterdam on Manhattan; it became the capital of New Netherland. Although the fur trade stimulated Dutch expansion into Delaware and the Hudson River Valley, farming was considered vital to making the colony self-sufficient. Under the **patroon system,** individuals who brought fifty settlers along with livestock and farm implements to the colony received large tracts of land.

Administration of New Netherland was in the hands of governors appointed by the Dutch West India Company. The colonists had little loyalty to these often corrupt and dictatorial officials, and when the English fleet appeared off Manhattan in 1664, no resistance was offered. This was not a sign that the Dutch welcomed English takeover, however. The two countries had been engaged in a series of wars for commercial supremacy; in fact, the Dutch won the colony back briefly during the Third Anglo-Dutch War in 1673. Nevertheless, New York, renamed for its new proprietor, James, Duke of York, became an English royal colony in 1685.

**New Jersey.** New Jersey was based on land grants made in 1664 by the Duke of York to Sir John Berkeley and Sir George Carteret, two of his favorite supporters. Small farming settlements that were in fact religious and ethnic enclaves of Anglicans, Puritans, Dutch Calvinists, Scottish Presbyterians, Swedish Lutherans, and Quakers predominated. The colony was divided into West and East Jersey by the proprietors in 1676 and was not reunited until 1702, when it reverted to direct royal control.

**Pennsylvania and Delaware.** William Penn received his proprietorship from Charles II in 1681, quite possibly as repayment of the debt the royal treasury owed his father. A member of the Society of Friends, or Quakers, he saw the grant as an opportunity to create a colony in North America—a "Peaceable Kingdom"—as a religious experiment.

The Quakers were looked upon with some suspicion in England because of their religious beliefs, but the sect thrived in spite of official persecution. They were pacifists, preached to the poor, refused to take oaths or tip their hats or bow to their social superiors, and gave women a role in the church. To encourage settlement, Penn actively promoted the attractions of Pennsylvania, not the least of which were religious toleration and good relations with the Indians based on Quaker pacifism and his willingness to buy rather than take Indian lands. The strategy worked, and the colony's population ballooned to more than eight thousand by 1700.

The first important settlement in Delaware was founded in 1638 by the New Sweden Company, a joint-stock company with Swedish and Dutch investors. But this Swedish outpost in the New World was short-lived. The colony first passed to the Dutch (1655), who could trace their claims to Henry Hudson's voyage, and then to England (1664). In 1682, Delaware was made part of William Penn's proprietorship and remained under the political control of the governor of Pennsylvania until the American Revolution.

**Georgia, the last English colony.** Georgia (named for George II) was carved out of territory originally part of South Carolina as a buffer against the Spanish in Florida and as a place where the poor of Europe could get a new start. The trustees to whom the land was granted, most important James Oglethorpe, envisioned a colony of prosperous small farmers and imposed regulations to bring this about. The land was given away, but no one could own more than five hundred acres, and the sale of land to other colonists or the bequeathing of farms to women heirs was prohibited. Slavery was also banned. While the trustees brought over anyone willing to work, making Georgia England's most cosmopolitan colony with German, Swiss, Austrian, Italian, and Jewish settlers, strong opposition to the landholding restrictions inevitably arose. All limitations were abolished by 1759, by which time Georgia was already a royal colony.

Although the colonists enjoyed a good deal of political autonomy through their elected assemblies (for example, the Virginia House of Burgesses and the Maryland House of Delegates), the colonies were part of the English imperial system. The **Navigation Acts,** first enacted by Parliament in 1660, regulated trade by requiring that goods be shipped on English ships with predominantly English crews and that certain commodities, called **enumerated articles,** be shipped to only England or its colonies. The laws reflected the economic policy known as **mercantilism,** which held that colonies exist for the benefit of the mother country as a source of raw materials and a market for its manufactured goods. On the international scene, the colonies could not escape the great power rivalry between England and France. Each of the wars fought between the two countries in Europe had its counterpart in North America.

## Colonial Society and Economy

By 1750, more than one million people, representing a population increase of significant proportions, were living in the thirteen colonies along the Atlantic coast. Disease, which had threatened the survival of many of the early settlements, was much reduced. Infant mortality rates in the colonies were much lower than those in England, and life expectancy was considerably higher. Women married earlier, giving them the opportunity to have more children, and large families were the norm. It was not uncommon at all for a woman to have eight children and more than forty grandchildren. Natural increase, the excess of live births over deaths, was important to the population growth, but ongoing European immigration was a factor as well. Whether refugees from war (the Germans, for example) or victims of persecution or economic conditions in their homelands (the Irish and Scotch-Irish), the new arrivals added to the ethnic and religious mosaic of eighteenth-century America. The largest ethnic group to arrive—the African slaves—came in chains.

**The expansion of slavery.** At midcentury, just under a quarter million blacks lived in the colonies, almost twenty times the number in 1700. The slave numbers increased, as had the white population, through a combination of immigration, albeit forced, and natural increase. As the supply of indentured servants diminished, in part because work opportunities had improved in England, the supply of slaves either imported directly from Africa or transshipped from the West Indies was increased. Charleston, South Carolina, and Newport, Rhode Island, were important points of entry. Competition from Brazilian and Caribbean planters kept the price of male field hands high, however, and the planters' North American counterparts responded by buying women and encouraging slave families.

The overwhelming majority of slaves lived in the southern colonies, but there was regional variation in distribution. In the Chesapeake area, slaveholding was far from universal, and many of the plantations had fewer than twenty slaves. A typical South Carolina planter, on the other hand, might own as many as fifty slaves to work in the rice fields. In some districts of the sparsely populated South Carolina colony, blacks outnumbered whites by as much as eight to one, and they were able to retain their African culture more than slaves who were taken to Virginia or Maryland. Although a mainstay of the southern economy, slavery was not unknown in the northern colonies. Slaves made up twenty percent of the population of New York in 1746, for example. Working as domestics, assistants to craftsmen, or stevedores in the port cities, they lived in their master's home, as did indentured servants and apprentices.

The slaves' resistance to their situation was often passive, involving feigning illness, breaking equipment, and generally disrupting the routine of the plantation, but it occasionally did turn violent. Given the demographics, it is not surprising that the largest colonial slave revolt—the **Stono Rebellion**—took place in South Carolina. In 1739, about one hundred fugitive slaves killed twenty whites on their way to Florida and were killed themselves when captured. The rebellion sparked other slave revolts over the next few years.

**Colonial agriculture.** The overwhelming majority of colonists were farmers. New England's rocky soil and short growing season along with the practice of dividing already small farms among siblings led families to a barely subsistent living. The crops they grew—barley, wheat, and oats—were the same as those grown in England, so they had little export value compared with the staples of the southern plantations. Many New Englanders left farming to fish or produce lumber, tar, and pitch that could be exchanged for English manufactured goods. In the Middle Colonies, richer land and a better climate created a small surplus. Corn, wheat, and livestock were shipped primarily to the West Indies from the growing commercial centers of Philadelphia and New York. Tobacco remained the most important cash crop around Chesapeake Bay, but the volatility of tobacco prices encouraged planters to diversify. Cereal grains, flax, and cattle became important to the economies of Virginia and Maryland in the eighteenth century. Rice cultivation expanded in South Carolina and Georgia, and indigo was added around 1740. The indigo plant was used to make a blue dye much in demand by the English textile industry.

Population growth put pressure on the limited supply of land in the north, while the best land in the south was already in the hands of planters. With opportunities for newcomers limited in the settled coastal areas, many German and Scotch-Irish immigrants pushed into the interior, where available land was more abundant. Filtering into the backcountry of Pennsylvania, Virginia, and the Carolinas, they established farms on the frontier and grew just enough food to keep themselves going.

**Colonial trade and industry.** The colonies were part of an Atlantic trading network that linked them with England, Africa, and the West Indies. The pattern of commerce, not too accurately called the **Triangular Trade,** involved the exchange of products from colonial farms, plantations, fisheries, and forests with England for manufactured goods and the West Indies for slaves, molasses, and sugar. In New England, molasses and sugar were distilled into rum, which was used to buy African slaves. Southern Europe was also a valuable market for colonial foodstuffs.

Colonial industry was closely associated with trade. A significant percentage of Atlantic shipping was on vessels built in the colonies, and shipbuilding stimulated other crafts, such as the sewing of sails, milling of lumber, and manufacturing of naval stores. Mercantile theory encouraged the colonies to provide raw materials for England's industrializing economy; pig iron and coal became important exports. Concurrently, restrictions were placed on finished goods. For example, Parliament, concerned about possible competition from colonial hatters, prohibited the export of hats from one colony to another and limited the number of apprentices in each hatmaker's shop.

**The social structure of the colonies.** At the bottom of the social ladder were slaves and indentured servants; successful planters in the south and wealthy merchants in the north were the colonial elite. In the Chesapeake area, the signs of prosperity were visible in brick and mortar. The rather modest houses of even the most prosperous farmers of the seventeenth century had given way to spacious mansions in the eighteenth century. South Carolina planters often owned townhouses in Charleston and would probably have gone to someplace like Newport to escape the heat in summer. Both in their lifestyles and social pursuits (such as horse racing), the southern gentry emulated the English country squire.

Large landholders were not confined just to the southern colonies. The descendants of the Dutch patroons and the men who received lands from the English royal governors controlled estates in the middle colonies. Their farms were worked by tenant farmers, who received a share of the crop for their labor. In the northern cities, wealth was increasingly concentrated in the hands of the merchants; below them was the middle class of skilled craftsmen and shopkeepers. Craftsmen learned their trade as apprentices and became journeymen when their term of apprenticeship (as long as seven years) was completed. Even as wage earners, the journeymen often still lived with their former master and ate at his table. Saving enough money to go into business for himself was the dream of every journeyman.

Among the urban poor were the unskilled laborers, stevedores, and crew members of the fishing and whaling fleets. Economic recessions were common in the colonies during the eighteenth century, and they affected workers in the cities most. When the supply of labor outstripped demand, wages fell and the level of unemployment rose.

By and large, women in the colonies assumed traditional roles; they took care of their home and brought up their children. On small farms throughout the colonies and in the backcountry, they also worked the fields and cared for livestock alongside their husbands and children. Urban women, freed from such domestic chores as spinning and candle making (cloth and candles could be purchased in the cities), had somewhat more leisure time, and they might help their husbands in their shop or tavern. Although women gave up their property rights when they married, single women and widows could inherit property under English law. It was not uncommon for a woman to manage her husband's business after his death. Midwifery, which required years of training, was the one profession open to women.

## Enlightenment and Religious Revival in the Colonies

Compared to England's literacy rate, that in the colonies was quite high. But while about half the colonists could read, their appetite for books rarely went beyond the Bible, the Book of Common Prayer, an almanac, and a volume of Shakespeare's plays. The better-educated elites among them were attuned to the new ideas that flowed into the port cities along with the products of English factories and the immigrants, including the ideas of the **Enlightenment.** Drawing on the Scientific Revolution, which had demonstrated that the physical world was governed by natural laws, men such as English philosopher John Locke argued that similar laws applied to human affairs and were discoverable through reason. Proponents of the Enlightenment also examined religion through the prism of reason. Rational Christianity, at its extreme, argued that God created the universe, established the laws of nature that made it work, and then did not interfere with the mechanism. This conception of God as a watchmaker is known as **deism.**

**Benjamin Franklin.** The Enlightenment in America was best represented by Benjamin Franklin, who clearly believed that the human condition could be improved through science. He founded the American Philosophical Society, the first truly scientific society in the colonies, and his academy grew into the University of Pennsylvania, the only college established in the eighteenth century that had no ties to a religious denomination. Franklin's new wood stove (1742) improved heating and ventilation in colonial homes, and his experiments with electricity led to the invention of the lightning rod (1752). Although a deist himself, Franklin was curious about the religious revival that swept through the colonies from the 1740s into the 1770s.

**The Great Awakening and its impact.** The Great Awakening grew out of the sense that religion was becoming an increasingly unimportant part of people's lives. In practical terms, this may well have been true. In Virginia, the most populous colony, the supply of ministers compared to the potential number of congregants was small, and churches in the backcountry were rare. The religious revival's leading figures were the Congregationalist minister Jonathan Edwards and the English evangelist George Whitefield, both dynamic preachers. Edwards was renowned for his "fire and brimstone" sermons that warned sinners about the fate God had in store for them if they did not repent. On numerous trips to the colonies beginning in 1738, Whitefield brought his message about the need for each individual to experience a "new birth" on the path to personal salvation (what today's fundamentalist Christians call being "born again").

In sharp contrast to the Enlightenment, the Great Awakening took on the proportions of a mass movement. Tens of thousands of people came to hear Whitefield preach as he moved from town to town, often holding meetings in the open or under tents, and he became a household name throughout the colonies. Moreover, the Great Awakening appealed to the heart, not the head. One of the reasons for its success was the emotion and drama that the revivalists brought to religion. The highlight of many of the services was the ecstatic personal testimony of those who had experienced a "new birth."

There is little doubt that the Great Awakening contributed to an increase in church membership and the creation of new churches. Congregations often split between the opponents ("Old Lights") and the supporters ("New Lights") of the religious revival. Slaves and Indians converted to Christianity in significant numbers for the first time, and the more evangelical sects, such as the Baptist and Methodist, grew. A rough estimate puts the number of religious organizations in the colonies in 1775 at more than three thousand. At the same time, the Great Awakening promoted religious pluralism. As the road to salvation was opened to everyone through personal conversion, doctrinal differences among the Protestant denominations became less important.

The religious movement is also often credited with encouraging the creation of new institutions of higher learning. Princeton University, founded as the College of New Jersey in 1746, grew out of the early revivalist William Tennent's Log College. Others established during the Great Awakening include Columbia University (King's College, 1754, Anglican), Brown University (Rhode Island College, 1764, Baptist), Rutgers (Queens College, 1766, Dutch Reformed), and Dartmouth College (1769, Congregationalist).

## Rivals for Empire

England was not the only country with territorial claims in North America. While Florida and vast stretches of the southwest from present-day Texas to California were under Spanish control, Spain did not pose a serious threat to English primacy. The only possible area of contention was in the southeast, and Georgia proved to be an effective buffer. France was another matter, however. The French controlled much of the land west of the Appalachians to the Rocky Mountains and south from the Great Lakes to the Gulf of Mexico. The handful of settlers from the colonies who ventured beyond the Appalachians quickly came into contact with French trappers and their Indian allies.

**The expansion of France in North America.** From their settlements in Canada (New France), the French expanded throughout the Great Lakes and into the Mississippi Valley in the late seventeenth century. In 1673, the Jesuit priest Jacques Marquette and the fur trader Louis Joliet traveled by land and canoe from what is today Wisconsin down the Mississippi River to its juncture with the Arkansas River. Nine years later, La Salle reached the Illinois River from Lake Michigan, followed it to its confluence with the Mississippi River, and from there explored the Mississippi to the Gulf of Mexico. He claimed the territory for France, naming the millions of acres that composed the Mississippi River watershed Louisiana in honor of King Louis XIV. French settlement of their newly claimed lands, however, did not begin in earnest until the eighteenth century. New Orleans was founded in 1718 as the capital of a colony that became a royal province in 1732, and French forts were established throughout the Mississippi, Missouri, and Ohio river valleys.

Marquette and Joliet reflected the principal motives behind French exploration and settlement: bringing Catholicism to the native tribes and expanding the fur trade. Neither motive was intended to bring large numbers of colonists to North America. Royal policy was an inhibiting factor to settlement as well. Louis XIV opened the French territory to only French Catholics; no place was made for French Huguenots, who had helped settle South Carolina, nor were there proprietors like William Penn who throughout Europe actively promoted the colonization of his land grant. As a result, the population of New France and Louisiana was quite small compared to that of the English colonies in the eighteenth century. Another important difference between the two was their relationship with the Indians. In the English colonies, disease, war, and slavery sum up the experience of the native tribes. French trappers, on the other hand, adopted Indian ways and often married Indian women. Although conversion was certainly the ultimate goal, even the Jesuit missionaries respected Indian culture. Most important, the size of the French presence posed no immediate threat to either the Indians' way of life or their lands. The Indians proved to be valuable allies of France in its conflicts with England.

**The wars between England and France.** Between 1689 and 1763, England and France fought four wars. The causes of each one, with the notable exception of the French and Indian War (the Seven Years' War, 1754–63), lay in European dynastic politics, and North America was a minor theater of operations.

While the outcome of **King William's War** (War of the League of Augsburg, 1689–97) was inconclusive, England acquired long-disputed territory in Canada through the Treaty of Utrecht, which ended **Queen Anne's War** (War of the Spanish Succession, 1702–13). Newfoundland, Acadia (which was later renamed Nova Scotia), and the fur-rich Hudson Bay were ceded to Great Britain. (Great Britain became the official name of England, Scotland, and Wales following their union in 1707.) The impact of the wars on the colonies, particularly New England, which supplied the bulk of the troops for the Canadian raids, was significant in loss of life, increased taxes, and debt. The third conflict between England and France, **King George's War** (War of the Austrian Succession, 1744–48), involved only minor border raids and skirmishes between the two countries and their Indian allies, without any meaningful results.

During the 1740s, fur traders from Pennsylvania and Virginia began to move into the Ohio River Valley; Virginia was also interested in land for its large and growing population, and several land companies received sizable grants from the Crown in 1749. The French responded by building a string of forts in the disputed territory, including Fort Duquesne near Pittsburgh. Hostilities began in 1754. George Washington, then a young officer in the Virginia militia, experienced his first defeat in the Pennsylvania backcountry at the hands of the French. When France and Great Britain decided to commit troops, the conflict on the frontier became a contest for the control of North America that soon had even wider international ramifications.

**The French and Indian War.** The first few years of the French and Indian War did not go well for the British. Despite their inferior numbers, the French had success relying on their considerable Indian support. The colonists and the British, on the other hand, were unable to persuade the **Six Nations**—a confederation of the Mohawk, Onandaga, Oneida, Cayuga, Seneca, and Tuscarora tribes—which had fought alongside them in previous conflicts, to end its neutrality. British commanders were ineffective, not understanding that tactics used on European battlefields were not effective in the wilderness. In hope of turning the tide, War Minister William Pitt mobilized the British army and navy for action in the colonies, despite the spread of the war to Europe (1756), and he agreed to reimburse the colonial legislatures for the cost of more American troops. The strategy worked. Fort Duquesne fell and the Iroquois joined the British in a series of successful campaigns along the northern New York frontier. The decisive battle in North America was at Quebec in 1759, where the fighting was so fierce that the opposing generals—Wolfe for the British and Montcalm for the French—were both killed. Montreal, the last important French stronghold in North America, was captured in 1760.

Although the war continued for another three years in the Caribbean and the Pacific, the outcome was never in doubt. Through the **Treaty of Paris** (1763), Britain acquired all French territory east of the Mississippi River and French Canada, with the exception of a few islands off the coast of Newfoundland. Spain, which had entered the war in 1761 on the side of France and had lost Cuba in the process, ceded Florida to the British to get the island back. France compensated Spain for the loss of Florida by giving up all its lands west of the Mississippi River, known as the Louisiana Territory.

In 1763, British power stretched from India to North America and the Caribbean, but the cost of creating the empire was high. Britain was facing an enormous postwar debt and already-high taxes as well as the need to finance the administration of its newly acquired lands. The British expected the American colonies, which prospered during the Seven Years' War through lucrative military contracts despite additional taxes, to assume at least part of the financial burden. The colonists had expectations as well: unfettered access to western lands, for example. Although most considered themselves English subjects and were proud to have helped Britain win an empire, a sense of American identity was developing. The colonists had gained greater control over their lives during the war, through their colonial assemblies' exacting concessions from royal governors as the price for raising revenue, and whether the colonists would again meekly accept the role of imperial subject was unknown.

## Discontent in the Colonies

The Seven Years' War had begun over control of the Ohio River Valley; affairs in that region became the first issue the British faced in governing their new empire. France's Indian allies certainly knew that the British victory meant more and more settlers would flood onto their lands. In the spring of 1763, Pontiac, an Ottawa leader, formed a coalition of tribes to drive the British off the western lands. **Pontiac's Rebellion** caused chaos in the Great Lakes region as his forces overran eight British forts and threatened both Detroit and Pittsburgh. The British fought back by giving Indians smallpox-infected blankets, an early example of biological warfare. Although Pontiac himself did not agree to peace until 1766, Parliament tried to placate the Indians through legislation.

**The Proclamation of 1763.** Intended to keep the colonists and Ohio Valley tribes separated as much as possible, the Proclamation of 1763 established a boundary running along the crest of the Appalachian Mountains. Unlicensed traders and settlers were banned west of the boundary. The colonists considered the proclamation a challenge to their land claims and continued pushing west, rendering its orders ineffective. Within a few years, British Indian agents negotiated treaties with the Iroquois, Cherokee, and other tribes, opening up large areas of western New York, Pennsylvania, Ohio, and Virginia to settlement.

The Proclamation of 1763 represented an attempt by Britain to exercise greater control over the colonies. The **Sugar Act,** passed by Parliament in 1764, had the same goal. For more than a century, the Navigation Acts had loosely regulated colonial trade to protect British commerce and manufacturing from competition; the duties imposed on the imports and exports were not intended to raise revenue. The Sugar Act reversed this policy; indeed, the law was officially called the American Revenue Act. By reducing the tax on molasses from the French West Indies and providing for stricter enforcement against smugglers through British vice-admiralty courts, Britain hoped to raise enough money to offset the cost of maintaining troops in the colonies.

**The Stamp Act.** The Stamp Act required the use of specially marked paper or the affixing of stamps on all wills, contracts, other legal documents, newspapers, and even playing cards. Any colonist who bought a newspaper or engaged in any business transaction was required to pay the tax, and violators faced severe penalties. In contrast to the duties charged under the Navigation Acts and even the Sugar Act, the Stamp Act charges represented the first internal tax, falling directly on the goods and services in the colonies.

Some British leaders, most notably William Pitt, objected strenuously to the Stamp Act because it raised the question of taxation without representation. Prime Minister George Grenville countered that all British subjects enjoyed **virtual representation;** that is, the members of Parliament represented not only the constituents of their district but the interests of British citizens everywhere, including those in America. The colonists, of course, sided with Pitt and claimed that if Americans were not sitting in Parliament, there was no way the members could know their concerns and interests.

**The colonial reaction to the Stamp Act.** To the colonists, the Stamp Act was a dangerous departure from previous policies, and they were determined to resist it. The Virginia House of Burgesses, led by Patrick Henry, passed resolutions against the legislation. Violent protests broke out in several of the colonies, led by groups calling themselves the Sons of Liberty. Stamp distributors were hung in effigy and suffered the destruction of their homes. In October 1765, representatives from nine colonies met as the **Stamp Act Congress,** which agreed that Parliament had the right to enact laws for the colonies but not to impose direct taxes. As the effective date of the Stamp Act approached (November 1, 1765), the colonists simply refused to use the stamps and organized an effective boycott of British goods. To prevent business from coming to a halt, royal officials backed away from requiring stamps on legal documents.

While Parliament was surprised by the extent of the colonial reaction, British manufacturers and merchants were distressed. Pointing out that the boycott could have serious economic repercussions at home, they demanded and got the repeal of the Stamp Act in March 1766. The revocation was more expedient than principled, and Parliament made it clear by passing the **Declaratory Act** on the same day that it still had the right to legislate for the colonies.

**The policies of Charles Townshend.** Charles Townshend became prime minister of Great Britain in 1767. He had opposed the Stamp Act, and the colonies initially hoped he would pursue more reasonable policies for North America. They were quickly disillusioned. Responding to protests in New York over the **Quartering** (or **Mutiny**) **Act of 1765,** which required colonial legislatures to pay for supplies needed by British troops, Townshend threatened to nullify all laws passed by the colony unless the payments were made. New York backed down but understood that the threat clearly interfered with colonial self-government. Townshend was just as committed as Grenville to raising revenues from the colonies. The Revenue Act of 1767, better known as the **Townshend duties,** taxed American imports of glass, lead, paper, paint, and tea. Because the new duties were external taxes unlike those of the Stamp Act, Townshend believed there would be little opposition; the colonists had moved beyond the distinction between internal and external taxes, however. John Dickinson, whose *Letters from a Farmer in Pennsylvania* was published in almost every newspaper in the colonies, argued that Parliament could not tax commerce for revenue purposes because that power resided in the colonial assemblies alone. Townshend had also created the American Board of Customs Commissioners to regulate the collection of the duties. Its soon-hated agents and commissioners used their office to enrich themselves by levying heavy fines for technical violations, to spy on alleged violators, and even to seize property for dubious reasons.

The Massachusetts House of Representatives circulated a letter, the **Massachusetts Circular Letter,** drafted by Samuel Adams, protesting Townshend's policies and again raising the issue of "no taxation without representation." When the letter was not rescinded, the legislature was dissolved by the royal governor on orders from London. A boycott again proved to be the most effective weapon the colonists wielded in their ongoing confrontation with Parliament. Merchants as well as consumers in Boston, New York, and Philadelphia and then throughout the colonies agreed not to import or use British goods. Colonial women joined the Daughters of Liberty, supporting the boycott by making their own thread and cloth. As a direct result of the boycott, the value of colonial imports from Britain dropped significantly from 1768 to 1769, a loss far exceeding the revenue generated by the Townshend duties. Parliament repealed the law for all goods except tea in 1770.

**The Boston Massacre.** Rioting in Boston over the actions of the Board of Customs Commissioners brought British soldiers to the city in October 1768. Over the next few years, animosity toward the soldiers grew and finally boiled over on March 5, 1770, when troops fired on a crowd of rock-throwing demonstrators, killing five. Although the soldiers had been provoked, and several were later brought to trial, patriots Samuel Adams and Paul Revere tried to use the incident to stir up anti-British passions. In fact, the "Boston Massacre" did not trigger further resistance, and tensions between the colonies and Britain eased, although temporarily.

## The Drift toward Revolution

Two events in 1772 brought the period of calm to an end. Rhode Island colonists burned the British ship *Gaspee,* which had run aground while patrolling for smugglers. Although the authorities ultimately found no one to prosecute, colonists learned that the plan had been to send the culprits to London for trial. At about the same time, the British government announced that the salaries of the Massachusetts governor and judges would henceforth be paid by the Crown, not the colonial legislature. Both incidents suggested that Britain was determined to undermine colonial liberties, and together they led to the formation of **committees of correspondence.** Created in Massachusetts to bring news of British abuses to town meetings, they promoted political education among the colonists and whipped up anti-British sentiment; by 1773, hundreds were operating nearly throughout the colonies.

**The Tea Act and Boston Tea Party.** In an attempt to rescue the almost bankrupt East India Company, Prime Minister Lord North gave the business a monopoly on the sale and distribution of tea in the colonies. The Tea Act (1773) lowered the price on tea to a point that not even the smugglers could match, and Parliament expected the colonists to welcome the windfall. North miscalculated the reaction to the tea monopoly just as Townshend had misjudged colonial reception of the external taxes. Revenue from the tea tax, despite the low price to consumers, cemented Parliament's right to tax the colonists, which was unacceptable to many Americans.

In Boston, colonists insisted that tea shipments be sent back to England without payment of the customs duties. When the governor refused, Bostonians, led by Samuel Adams, took matters into their own hands. Fifty men disguised as Mohawk Indians boarded one of the ships and threw the entire cargo of tea into the harbor. The **Boston Tea Party** (December 16, 1773) was a crucial turning point. The colonists had moved beyond boycotts to the destruction of property, and as far as Lord North and King George III were concerned, the new issue was whether and how Britain would regain control over the colonies.

**The Coercive Acts.** In response to the Boston Tea Party, Parliament passed a series of punitive measures against Massachusetts. The **Coercive Acts** (called the **Intolerable Acts** in the colonies) closed the port of Boston until the cost of the tea and customs charges were repaid; revoked parts of the Massachusetts charter, letting the king select members for the legislature's upper house and the governor appoint most officials; and allowed British troops and royal officials accused of a capital offense while carrying out their duties to be tried in another colony or in England. A new **Quartering Act,** which applied to all the colonies, permitted the governors to house soldiers in private houses or buildings. Around the same time, Parliament enacted the **Quebec Act,** which recognized Catholicism as the official religion of Quebec. The act was an affront to Protestant Anglo-Americans, particularly in New England. More important, the Ohio River was made the southern boundary of Quebec, taking territory that Massachusetts, Virginia, and Connecticut claimed.

Clearly, the Coercive Acts were aimed not just at Massachusetts but all the colonies. Prior loosely coordinated colonial responses to English laws were judged to be inadequate this time, and calls went out for a meeting of representatives to develop a joint plan of action. Twelve of the thirteen colonies (only Georgia did not send a delegation) participated in the **First Continental Congress** in Philadelphia during September and October 1774.

**The First Continental Congress.** Although the representatives attending the First Continental Congress endorsed the Massachusetts **Suffolk Resolves,** a set of statements which in addition to condemning the Coercive Acts called on the colonists to form their own militias, the final declaration adopted by the Congress was considerably more moderate. The grievances and resolves were essentially a condemnation of Parliament for denying the colonists the rights and privileges they traditionally enjoyed as English subjects. In matters of taxation and internal policy, the colonies, through their legislatures, were free to chart their own course, subject only to a veto by the king. The declaration sought the repeal of all legislation enacted since 1763 that ran counter to this basic principle, including the Intolerable Acts, and a redress of their grievances by appealing not to Parliament but to the Crown and the British people. The Congress was clearly not prepared to completely break with Britain.

To specifically fight the Coercive Acts, the representatives agreed to suspend all economic ties—imports, exports, and consumption—with Great Britain. While several colonies had already approved non-importation agreements, the economic plan was significant in several respects. First, it included a ban on the importation of slaves, not out any moral concern over the evils of slavery but because of the impact a ban would have on the British slave-trade monopoly. Second, the boycott was to be enforced through the committees of correspondence operating under rules set by the newly created Continental Association.

## The Start of the American Revolution

Some hoped the colonies could put enough economic pressure on Great Britain to prevent the crisis from escalating. Imports dropped by more than ninety percent from 1774 to 1775, and English merchants were appealing to Parliament to compromise with the colonies as early as January 1775. William Pitt in the House of Lords and Edmund Burke in the House of Commons also urged reconciliation, and Lord North was developing his own plan. But events in Massachusetts were moving quickly toward armed conflict.

**Lexington and Concord.** General Thomas Gage, the military governor of Massachusetts, began fortifying Boston in the fall of 1774; colonists meanwhile prepared militias, organizing small, armed groups ready for quick action as **Minute Men.** In the spring, Gage was ordered to arrest radical leaders and put down what was considered to be an open rebellion in the colony, despite the discussions underway in Parliament. To warn of the impending movement of British troops, William Dawes and Paul Revere rode out to alert the local townspeople and farmers. On April 19, colonials and British soldiers faced each other on the town green at Lexington. Shots were fired, leaving eight colonists dead. The British continued on to Concord, where militia supplies were stored, and confronted another group of Americans, exchanging fire. Colonists continued to harass the British as they marched backed to Boston, killing or wounding 273 by the end of the engagement.

The rebellion quickly spread. The British garrison in Boston was besieged, and the Green Mountain Boys of Vermont, led by Ethan Allen, captured Fort Ticonderoga with the intention of using its cannon in Boston. The Battle of Bunker Hill (June 17, 1775), the first major confrontation of the American Revolution, was a British victory but at the cost of more than a thousand men. The Second Continental Congress met in Philadelphia as the fighting raged.

**The Second Continental Congress.** The outbreak of hostilities still did not mean the colonies were prepared to declare their independence. Indeed, the Second Continental Congress adopted the **Olive Branch Petition,** professing loyalty to the Crown and appealing to George III to end the bloodshed so outstanding issues between the colonies and Great Britain could be worked out. Even the statement justifying the taking up of arms rejected independence as a solution, though it underscored the colonists' commitment to fight for their rights. Nevertheless, circumstances dictated that the Congress assume governmental responsibilities: a letter was sent to Canada asking for its support, or at least neutrality, in the fighting; the troops around Boston were declared a Continental Army, and George Washington was named commander; approval was given for the appointment of commissioners to negotiate treaties with the Indians and for the establishment of a postal service.

By the time the Second Continental Congress reopened in September, George III had rejected the Olive Branch Petition, and New England was proclaimed in a state of rebellion. In December, Parliament closed the colonies to all trade. For its part, the Congress created a navy and sounded out the European powers on their position toward the colonies. France, not surprisingly, eventually became a critical ally for the Americans.

**The balance of forces.** At first glance, Great Britain appeared to have enormous advantages over the colonies. The British had a professional army, eventually putting more than one hundred thousand men in the field along with thirty thousand German (Hessian) mercenaries. These troops were well armed, supplied, and trained. Britain could draw on vast economic resources and had the largest navy in the world, but it did face serious problems. Supplying their forces in the colonies and communicating effectively with commanders across an ocean were difficult. The cost of war meant still higher taxes for a country saddled with debts from previous conflicts. It was an open question just how long the British would continue paying to keep the colonies in the empire.

The Americans were fighting on their soil for their own liberties and, in short order, their independence, all advantages to their side. George Washington, in spite of his limited military experience, proved to be an adept leader. Compromising his ability to lead the more than two hundred thousand men who fought in the war were the poorly trained and undisciplined militias. In addition, food, medicine, and ammunition were often in short supply because the Continental Congress had no power to compel the colonies to provide what was needed. Nor did the colonies fulfill their quotas for troops for the Continental Army. Perhaps the most serious handicap was the significant number of Americans who not only opposed the war but sided with the British.

**Loyalists versus Patriots.** British sympathizers were called **Loyalists** or **Tories;** backers of the fight against England were known as **Whigs** or **Patriots.** An estimated twenty percent of Americans, unevenly distributed throughout the colonies, supported Great Britain. The Loyalists included government officials whose positions and livelihoods were tied to the empire, merchants who were dependent on British trade (New York City was a Loyalist stronghold), and those who believed that a break with Britain would lead to instability or chaos. Among the last group were people who had actively opposed the Stamp Act and signed nonimportation agreements but felt that revolution was going too far. About twenty-one thousand Loyalists fought with the British, and five times that number decided to leave the country at the end of hostilities. In a very real sense, the American Revolution was a civil war.

Native Americans, including most of the powerful Iroquois nation, supported the British, for obvious reasons. During the long-standing dispute over western lands, it was Great Britain that had issued the protective Proclamation of 1763, while the Americans increasingly moved onto Indian lands. Slaves also joined the British because they were promised their freedom; escaped slaves served in the British army as soldiers and laborers.

Although the Second Continental Congress increasingly assumed the powers of an independent government, the decision to formally declare independence was not made until more than a year after the fighting had begun. Indeed, colonial officers toasted the good health of the king at dinners. Throughout the crisis that led to the revolution, it was not the king but Parliament and the king's ministers who were blamed for causing the rift between the colonies and Great Britain. In time, though, a dramatic change in attitude toward George III transformed the American Revolution into a war for independence.

## The War for Independence

In January 1776, Thomas Paine, who had come to America from England hardly more than a year earlier, published a pamphlet titled *Common Sense,* which was a clear call for independence. Paine's theme was not corrupt politics but the struggle between liberty and monarchy in the person of George III. The pamphlet was a huge success—more than one hundred thousand copies were quickly in circulation—and provided the impetus needed for most Americans to favor independence. In the months that followed its publication, the colonial legislatures were replaced with new state governments that approved a final break with Great Britain.

**The Declaration of Independence.** In June 1776, a committee appointed by the Continental Congress took up the task of drafting a declaration of independence. Its members included Thomas Jefferson (the principal author), John Adams, and Benjamin Franklin. The Congress first voted for independence on July 2 and then discussed the document Jefferson had prepared, making a significant change during the debates. Jefferson's attack on slavery and the slave trade was stricken from the draft at the insistence of South Carolina, Georgia, and some of the representatives from the northern states. The notion that "all men are created equal" clearly did not apply to blacks. The Declaration of Independence, as amended, was adopted on July 4, 1776, affirming the vote taken two days earlier.

The Declaration of Independence is an itemized list of grievances against the misrule and abuses of George III; Parliament is not mentioned. Jefferson drew heavily on the political philosophy of the Enlightenment, particularly John Locke's contract theory of government. His main points were that people have natural rights—the "unalienable rights" of "life, liberty, and the pursuit of happiness"—and that governments are created to protect those rights; when a government, whose authority stems from the consent of the people, attempts to destroy those rights, the people can and should abolish it.

**Fighting the war.** The main theaters of fighting shifted during the course of the war from New England (1775–76) to the middle states (1776–78) to the southern states (1778–82). In the spring of 1776, the British left Boston and moved their military headquarters to New York City, where they had the advantages of an excellent harbor, ample food supplies, and Loyalist support. George Washington also moved his forces south but was defeated in major engagements on Long Island and Manhattan. He retreated from New York in the fall, convinced he needed to adopt more innovative tactics. During the eighteenth century, armies usually retired to winter quarters and resumed their campaigns in the spring. On Christmas in 1776, however, the Americans surprised the Hessian garrison at Trenton by crossing the Delaware River in a daring night raid. This victory was quickly followed by a successful attack on Princeton on January 3. Both battles were important in raising American morale.

Another major victory occurred in October 1777 at Saratoga in upper New York state. Taking advantage of a series of blunders, the Continental Army defeated the British forces under General Burgoyne, which included significant numbers of Loyalists and Indians, and took more than five thousand prisoners. Burgoyne and American General Horatio Gates agreed that the British troops would lay down their arms and return to England, pledging not to serve in the war again, but this compact was never implemented. The true significance of the Battle of Saratoga is that France was persuaded to become an ally of the Americans.

**Diplomacy during the war.** The Americans realized that the war for independence would be lost without the support of other nations. Indeed, they had looked to France as a potential ally in the struggle with Great Britain as early as 1774. In late 1776, with both France and Spain already secretly providing munitions and money for the war, a delegation led by Benjamin Franklin went to Paris hoping to negotiate a formal alliance.

Franklin was a popular figure at the French court, but it took news of Saratoga before France recognized the United States as a sovereign nation. A commercial agreement and a formal alliance, which actually became effective when France and England went to war in June, were concluded. French aid ultimately tipped the balance in favor of the Americans. In addition to providing direct assistance in the form of men and ships, the French alliance forced Britain to bolster its troops in other parts of the empire, spreading its forces even more thinly.

Spain declared war on Britain in 1779 but did not recognize the United States; the Dutch Republic did the same in 1780. The combined French, Spanish, and Dutch fleets outnumbered the British warships. Catherine the Great of Russia created the League of Armed Neutrality, a coalition of European states that followed a policy of passive hostility toward Great Britain. The British had to deal with Russia and Sweden in 1780 and Prussia and Portugal in 1782. These diversions were costly and helped make the American war increasingly impractical in both economic and political terms.

**Winning the war.** By enduring several major defeats and surviving the harsh winter encampments at Valley Forge (1777–78), the Continental Army matured into a disciplined fighting force. The British no longer won easy victories over poorly trained American troops. In

1778, when the war expanded to the west and south, George Rogers Clark moved into the Ohio Valley and fought several battles against the British and their Loyalist and Indian allies. Hoping to take advantage of Loyalist sentiment, the British turned their attention south in late 1778. The strategy was to take Georgia and South Carolina and then move north to Virginia, but after capturing Savannah and Charleston, major port cities, the British found controlling the interior much more difficult. Then, in 1781, the British made a fatal strategic mistake. General Lord Cornwallis set up a base at Yorktown in Virginia, intending to press the campaign into Virginia and Pennsylvania. Yorktown was located on a peninsula; when the French fleet blockaded by sea and a combined force of American and French troops laid siege to the city, Cornwallis was cut off. While skirmishes continued, the war was effectively over when Cornwallis and his eight thousand soldiers laid down their arms on October 19, 1781.

**The Peace of Paris.** In June 1782, an American delegation led by Benjamin Franklin, John Adams, and John Jay opened peace talks with British and French diplomats in Paris. Several issues complicated the peace conference. France wanted all the parties involved to sign the treaty, and, indeed, the Americans had been instructed by Congress not to sign a separate agreement. Jay ignored his instructions when it became clear that France wanted to limit the United States to the territory east of the Appalachians.

Through the Peace of Paris, Great Britain recognized the independence of the United States with the Mississippi River as its western boundary. Americans were granted fishing rights off Newfoundland and Nova Scotia, and British troops and ships were to depart from American territory "with all convenient speed." Left unresolved, however, were issues that damaged Anglo-American relations for years. The United States agreed to compensate Loyalists for property confiscated during the war, but the new government lacked the power to compel the states to do so; the British refused to leave several military outposts until this matter was resolved. The fate of the tribes that had fought with the British was omitted from the treaty; Native Americans in the Ohio Valley refused to recognize the sovereignty of the United States, leaving open the potential for further conflict. The British also did nothing for the luckless slaves who had sided with them.

## Governing the New Nation

After eight years of war preceded by more than a decade of political uncertainty and crisis, the United States had won its independence. With peace, it faced the challenge of working out the most effective and practical means of governing itself and the proper relationship between the national government and the states, a task that had begun while the war was still being fought.

**New state governments.** The colonial governments collapsed when the war broke out. The royal governors fled, and in eleven of the thirteen states, revolutionary conventions took it upon themselves to write new constitutions. Almost all provided for a strong two-house legislature that, in most of the states, could elect the state's governor. A general distrust of executive authority made for weak governors; frequently, they might serve only a one-year term, could not veto laws, and were not free to make appointments without the approval of the legislature. Property qualifications for both voting and holding an office were the rule, meaning the franchise was limited to a portion of each state's white males. The new state governments were not democratic in the modern sense because "democracy" in the eighteenth century was associated with mob rule, something that was feared just as much as oppressive monarchy. On the other hand, many of the states included a bill of rights in their constitution to protect basic liberties.

**The Articles of Confederation.** The first national government was created through the Articles of Confederation, a document adopted by the Second Continental Congress in November 1777. It went into effect when ratified by all the states in March 1781. During the intervening period, the business of government and the conducting of war were carried out by the Continental Congress. The delay in moving from a provisional to a permanent government was caused by a dispute among the states over western lands. Massachusetts, New York, and Virginia claimed their western boundaries were the Mississippi River, which was disputed by other states. Maryland in particular feared the potential size and power of New York and Virginia and did not ratify the Articles until 1781, when the claims were relinquished.

Under the Articles of Confederation, the national government consisted of a **unicameral** (one-house) legislature, often called the Confederation Congress. There was no national executive or judiciary. Delegates to Congress were appointed by the state legislatures, and each state had one vote, regardless of the number of its delegates. Nine votes were needed to pass a law, or **ordinance,** as it was called then. Amending the Articles required a unanimous vote. Congress had the power to declare war, develop foreign policy, coin money, regulate Native-American affairs in the territories, run the post office, borrow money, and appoint officers to the army and navy. Quite significantly, all powers not specifically given to Congress belonged to the states.

The Articles had several weaknesses. Congress could not tax the states; when funds were needed for whatever purpose, it could ask the states for money but could not compel them to pay. Nor could Congress regulate interstate or foreign trade, and the states, in fact, had the right to impose their own duties on imports, which played havoc with commerce. And although Congress could declare war, it had no authority to raise an army on its own; it had to requisition troops from the states.

**Finance and Shays's Rebellion.** When the war ended, the United States was $160 million in debt. To meet the need for a national currency, Congress printed paper money backed by European loans. More money was printed than the value of the loans, however, and its worth plunged while inflation shot up. The problem of paying off its debts plagued the new nation. Army officers even threatened to mutiny unless they were given their back pay.

Inflation was also a serious problem for the states, which printed their own money. High taxes along with the refusal of creditors to accept paper money led to an increasing number of farm foreclosures, triggering social unrest. Daniel Shays, a captain during the American Revolution and a farmer who had fallen on hard times himself, led two thousand men on a campaign to shut down courthouses (where foreclosure documents were issued) in several Massachusetts counties. Concern mounted when Shays marched on Springfield, the site of an arsenal, but the farmers and veterans that joined him were easily dispersed by the militia. Shays's Rebellion caused the Massachusetts legislature to reduce taxes and exempt personal items, such as household goods and tools, from seizure in a foreclosure.

**Achievements of the Confederation Congress.** Despite its political and economic shortcomings, the Confederation Congress achieved some notable successes, especially in the administration of western lands. The **Ordinance of 1785** created a basic system for surveying land. Surveys established townships of six square miles and divided them into thirty-six sections of 640 acres. In turn, each section was divided into half sections (320 acres) or quarter sections (160 acres). The government calculated that a family of four could live independently on a 160-acre farm, a concept that endured well into the twentieth century. One of the thirty-six sections in each township was reserved to be a source of income for public education.

The **Northwest Ordinance of 1787** established the Northwest Territory (eventually the states of Ohio, Indiana, Illinois, Wisconsin, and Michigan) and outlined the process by which almost all territories have become states. When a territory was organized, Congress first appointed a territorial governor and judges. When five thousand adult males lived in the territory, a territorial legislature was elected and a temporary constitution written. When the total population reached sixty thousand, a state constitution was prepared, and the territorial residents petitioned Congress for admission to the union as a state.

**Frontier and foreign policy problems.** The Northwest Ordinance pledged that Native Americans' land and property would not be taken without their consent. In fact, the treaties by which the United States acquired Indian lands were often negotiated under duress. U.S. commissioners, for example, refused to recognize the Six Nations and insisted on dealing with individual Iroquois tribes. Most of the tribes repudiated the treaties and openly resisted the expansion of settlements. By 1786, fighting was common along the Ohio River frontier, involving the Shawnee, Delaware, Wyandotte, and Miami tribes, and had broken out in Georgia with the Creek. Spain added to the problems in the southeast by encouraging the Creek. Alexander McGillivray, the Creek leader, won some concessions by playing one country against the other. The inability of the Confederation Congress to maintain peace on the frontier added to calls for a stronger national government.

As its reward for joining with France against Great Britain, Spain regained East and West Florida, which it had lost to the British after the Seven Years' War. The Spanish claimed that the boundary of West Florida extended to the Mississippi River, so it was able to close the port of New Orleans to American shipping in 1784. The shutdown was a severe blow to farmers in the trans-Appalachian territory. Lacking roads across the mountains, they could get their crops to market only by traveling down the Mississippi. The attempt to work out the problem through the **Jay-Gardoqui Treaty,** which would have denied the United States navigation rights on the lower Mississippi for twenty-five years but opened Spanish markets to East Coast merchants, failed completely. Pressure from southern and western farmers made it unlikely that Congress would have ratified the agreement. The issue was not resolved until 1789 when access to New Orleans was finally achieved.

## Drafting the Constitution

A combination of factors underscored the need for a stronger national government than the Articles of Confederation provided. American manufacturing was stunted because Congress had no power to impose high tariffs to protect domestic industry from foreign competition. Settlers in the west demanded a more aggressive policy on land cessions and that more be done to protect them from Indian attacks. Merchants were looking for a government that could negotiate favorable international trade agreements. While modifying the Articles was not considered particularly urgent among the southern and mid-Atlantic states, even their leaders appreciated that free navigation of the Mississippi River and a resolution of the dispute with Spain required a response from a stronger government.

**The Constitutional Convention.** In May 1787, fifty-five delegates from twelve of the thirteen states (Rhode Island did not attend) met in Philadelphia. Among them were George Washington (chosen as the chair), Benjamin Franklin, James Madison, and Alexander Hamilton. As a group, the delegates were men in their thirties and forties, many were lawyers, and most had served in Congress. Although the stated purpose of the Convention was to "revise" the Articles of Confederation, the participants quickly moved to develop a new structure of government.

**The Virginia and New Jersey plans.** The early constitutional debates focused on a proposal submitted by James Madison that became known as the **Virginia plan,** or **"large-state" plan.** It called for a bicameral legislature empowered to make laws and levy taxes with the representation in both houses based on population. Members of the lower house would be elected by voters in each state, and members of the upper house would be chosen by the lower house from candidates nominated by the state legislatures. The plan had no provision for electing an executive; the president would be chosen by the national legislature to serve for one term and was responsible for executing all laws. The legislature would also appoint judges to one or more supreme courts and lower national courts.

Opposition to Madison's proposal developed immediately. William Paterson of New Jersey, noting that the large-state plan would give considerable power to states like Virginia and New York, offered a less radical departure from the Articles of Confederation. The **New Jersey plan,** or **"small-state" plan,** kept the one-house legislature of the Confederation Congress but expanded its powers to include raising revenue and regulating commerce. The members were chosen by the state legislatures and each state was given one vote. A multi-person executive elected by the legislature was proposed. The executives, who were removable by action of the majority of the governors, also appointed judges to a supreme court. Laws passed by the legislature were binding on the states, and the multiperson executive was authorized to compel obedience to the law.

**The Great Compromise.** The New Jersey Plan was rejected, but the apportionment of representation in Congress continued to divide the Constitutional Convention. The large states wanted proportional representation (based on population), and the small states demanded equal representation (one state, one vote). The solution to the dilemma came through the **Great Compromise** (also known as the **Connecticut Compromise**), which made the number of seats in the House of Representatives proportional to each state's population and each representative elected directly by the people. In the Senate, each state would have two independently voting senators to be chosen by the state legislatures.

**Slavery and the presidency.** The issue of whether or how to count slaves in each state's population was resolved by a formula used by the Confederation Congress in 1783. For purposes of representation in the House and assessing direct taxes to the states, population was determined by the "whole number of free persons" and "three fifths of all other persons." The phrase "all other persons" meant slaves. In addition to the **Three-Fifths Compromise,** the delegates allowed the slave trade to continue, by denying Congress the power to prohibit it before 1808, and agreed that fugitive slaves should be returned to their masters.

The Convention accepted a one-person executive but hotly debated how the president should be elected—by Congress or by the people. Election of the executive was resolved through the invention of the **Electoral College.** The state legislatures would choose the same number of **electors** as their total number of representatives in Congress, and the electors would vote for two presidential candidates. The candidate who received the most votes would become president and the person with the next highest total would become vice president. In the event of a tie, the election would be decided by the House of Representatives, each state having one vote in this situation.

Other mechanisms of the new government were hammered out during the Convention. The Constitution provides for the **separation of powers**, meaning that governmental functions are in the hands of the executive, legislative, and judicial branches, and that a system of **checks and balances** ensures that one branch does not dominate the others. For example, the president can veto laws passed by Congress, but Congress can override the veto by a two-thirds vote. Foreign policy is in the hands of the president, but the Senate must approve all treaties.

**Ratifying the Constitution.** A minimum of nine states was needed to ratify the Constitution. In the months after the Convention finished its work (September 1787), the debate over ratification raged in newspapers, in pamphlets, and on the floors of state legislatures. To educate voters and stimulate public discussion, Alexander Hamilton, James Madison, and John Jay wrote a series of essays supporting the strong government provided for in the Constitution, which were published in papers across the country. The articles are collectively known as the *Federalist Papers,* and those who favored ratification of the new constitution called themselves **Federalists.** Their opponents went by the rather awkward name of **Antifederalists,** believing that the new document gave too much power to the national government and left the states too little. Staunch proponents of individual liberty, they strongly attacked the omission of a bill of rights, already included in many state constitutions.

On June 21, 1788, New Hampshire became the ninth state to rat-ify the Constitution. Virginia and New York, crucial because of their size and influence, narrowly approved it five days later. Rhode Island, on the other hand, waited until May 29, 1790, to take action, but by that time, the government was already operating under the Constitu-tion. The last holdout states could hardly afford to stay out of the new nation.

George Washington was inaugurated the first president of the United States on April 30, 1789, seven weeks late because many newly elected senators and congressmen were delayed in reaching New York, the country's first capital. The new nation had no real road system, and travel was slow. The administration lost no time, however, in setting up the framework for a national government.

## Organizing the Government

The Constitution as ratified failed to address several important issues. It did not formally protect basic civil liberties, even though many state constitutions contained such provisions, and it left the structure of the executive branch vague. The president was given the power to appoint officials, and mention is made of "the principal officer in each of the executive departments," but which departments and what their functions might be are not spelled out. The first omission was addressed through the amendment process, while the actual practice of government took care of the second.

**Unfinished business: the Bill of Rights and the first cabinet.** In ratifying the Constitution, five states had insisted on adding provisions to protect the people against governmental abuse. The new Congress thus appointed a committee to consider possible amendments to the Constitution, which collectively became known as the Bill of Rights. Under the leadership of James Madison, seventeen were originally proposed; they were reduced to twelve by the Senate; ten were eventually ratified by the states.

The most fundamental concerns were incorporated into the First Amendment: freedom of religion, speech, and the press and the right to peaceably assemble and to petition the government for a redress of grievances. The Second Amendment guaranteed that the states could form their own militias—forerunners of the modern National Guard units—and, in a somewhat vague fashion, that people could keep and bear arms. The Third Amendment prevented soldiers from being quartered in private homes, which had been a grievance against British practices even before the War for Independence. The Fourth Amendment protected people from unreasonable search and seizure; the Fifth shielded them from self-incrimination; the Sixth pledged citizens a speedy trial; the Seventh ensured a trial by jury. Excessive bail and cruel and unusual punishment were prohibited by the Eighth Amendment. The Ninth Amendment made certain that a right's not being specifically mentioned in the Constitution was not grounds for it to be denied to the people. The tenth and last amendment reserved certain rights to the states and people.

There is no provision in the Constitution for a cabinet, but the term became popular in the 1790s to describe the group of executive officers that advises the president. The executives would likely have met with the president in a small, private room, or cabinet. The first cabinet members were the secretaries of state, treasury, and war, and the attorney general. Washington asked Thomas Jefferson to be secretary of state and Alexander Hamilton to serve as secretary of the treasury. The two distinguished statesmen soon found themselves in fundamental disagreement over issues larger than those specific to their offices.

**Hamilton's reports.** The United States was saddled with a large debt from the War for Independence. Hamilton submitted recommendations for dealing with the problem in his **"Report on the Public Credit"** (January 1790). It called for funding the national debt by printing new securities and honoring at face value the certificates that had been issued by the Continental Congress. In addition, he proposed that the federal government assume state debts. Hamilton did not intend for the national debt to be totally eliminated; paying the interest would be enough to demonstrate the financial viability of the new nation.

Hamilton's report aroused concern from the southern states, whose leaders believed the proposal primarily benefited speculators in the north. James Madison noted that many of the original certificate owners—farmers and veterans, for the most part—had long ago sold their certificates at deep discounts because they were considered almost worthless; current holders stood to make a huge profit. Hamilton bought the southern leaders' consent for assumption of state debts by supporting the creation of a new national capital site in Virginia and Maryland (the District of Columbia). Congress approved the "Report on the Public Credit" (August 1790), and the financial benefit to the United States was virtually immediate.

In December, Hamilton issued his **"Report on a National Bank"** to Congress. It was approved two months later, creating a federally chartered bank, mostly under private control, that would handle federal deposits, make loans to the government when necessary, and issue paper notes in lieu of scarce hard cash. It would also enrich shareholders, another positive outcome in light of Hamilton's view that a prosperous elite was essential for the success of the nation.

Hamilton followed the national bank report with his **"Report on Manufactures"** in December 1791. He called for protective tariffs on imports to encourage domestic manufacturing. The report even approved of child labor. Congress did not support his high tariff, but Hamilton achieved the same result by charging higher duties on goods imported on non-American ships than on American ships, an action benefiting the growth of the U.S. merchant marine.

**Opposition to Hamilton's plans.** Thomas Jefferson became the acknowledged leader of the growing political opposition to Hamilton's policies. Their differences were rooted in competing visions of America. Hamilton saw a country rich in urban, merchant, financial, and in time, manufacturing interests. Jefferson saw the United States as a land for yeoman farmers. The two factions evolved into political parties that by 1796 were called Federalist and Republican (the latter not to be confused with the modern Republican party). The term **"Federalist"** is misleading because Federalist party supporters actually favored a strong central government; a true federal system would have given much more power to the states. Jeffersonian **Republicans** advocated low tariffs to benefit an agrarian society and a relatively weak national government. They also favored a strong relationship with France, then in the midst of its revolution, while the Federalists wanted economic and political ties with Great Britain.

Federalists and Republicans also differed in their interpretation of the Constitution. Hamilton made much of the so-called **"elastic clause"** in the Constitution (Article I, Section 8), which authorizes Congress to make all laws "necessary and proper" to carry out its enumerated powers. The creation of the national bank is a pertinent example of its use. Jefferson and the Republicans, on the other hand, favored a "strict interpretation" of the Constitution; that is, if the Constitution didn't specifically indicate something could be done, it could not be done. Taken to its extreme, this position would hamper the ability of the government to deal with issues that the founders never envisioned. Jefferson himself recognized this when he became president. Although there is no authority in the Constitution for the acquisition of territory from another country, he went ahead with the Louisiana Purchase (1803) because it was too great a bargain to pass up.

**The Whiskey Rebellion.** The first major test of the authority of the national government came from western Pennsylvania. Isolated from the east coast by the Appalachian Mountains, farmers in the region faced the serious problem of not being able to market their crops. New Orleans, under Spanish control, was still closed to American traffic. Because they could not ship their corn and rye down the Ohio and Mississippi rivers, the farmers instead distilled the grains into liquor. By reducing the size of their crop, they both enhanced its value and made transport to market across the mountains by pack train possible.

Under Hamilton, an excise was imposed on whiskey amounting to twenty-five percent of the product's retail value, effectively erasing all of the farmers' profit. Moreover, anyone accused of evading the tax had to go at his own expense to Philadelphia for trial. Western

Pennsylvania farmers were particularly incensed because they seemed to be the main targets of the tax, as it was not evenly enforced in all areas.

In July 1794, the Whiskey Rebellion broke out as farmers declared their defiance of the law and rioted against tax officials, burning buildings and even calling for secession from the United States. President Washington promptly ordered the militias of Pennsylvania, Maryland, Virginia, and New Jersey to march against the rebels. Opposition quickly evaporated against this combined force of almost thirteen thousand men. Of the one hundred fifty arrested, only two were actually convicted of treason, and Washington later pardoned both of them. The point had been clearly made, however: federal law was to be obeyed, and violent protest, a method successfully employed against British policies two decades earlier, would not be tolerated.

## Foreign Policy Challenges

In matters of foreign policy, the new nation faced a combination of unresolved issues and new political problems. Despite Great Britain's promises to evacuate frontier outposts, British soldiers had remained there for more than ten years. Native Americans looked for alliances with Great Britain and Spain to curtail American westward expansion. Across the Atlantic, the French Revolution sparked wars against Great Britain and Spain and tested U.S. neutrality policies.

**Conflicts on the frontier.** When Washington took office, the ongoing conflict between the tribes in the Ohio Valley and white settlers demanded a solution. American military expeditions against the Miami Confederacy (an alliance of eight western tribes) in 1790 and 1791 both failed. Washington called for a third expedition, led by General Anthony Wayne, a veteran of the American Revolution who knew how to temper bravery with caution. Great Britain, which incited the tribes in hopes of maintaining a British presence in the

Northwest Territory, did not provide any direct aid. Wayne's well-trained and well-supplied force of more than two thousand men won a major victory in the Battle of Fallen Timbers (August 1794). Through the Treaty of Greenville, twelve of the western tribes yielded almost all of present-day Ohio, part of Indiana, and sites for sixteen trading posts. Native-American resistance in the region came to an end for almost twenty years.

U.S. relations with the southeastern tribes were different. Washington successfully negotiated with the Cherokee, Creek, and Choctaw without recourse to war, even though Indian leaders in the region, most notably Creek Chief Alexander McGillivray, played the Spaniards against the Americans, and President Washington knew it. The Creek especially were hostile toward settlers in Georgia, who were encroaching on their tribal lands. Washington concluded the Treaty of New York in 1790, promising that the Creek's territorial rights would be respected and that Georgia would restore lands to their allies, the Chickasaw and Choctaw.

**Problems with France.** The French Revolution had initially been greeted with enthusiasm by the United States, but by 1793 many Americans were upset by the direction the revolution had taken. The French not only executed their king and queen but also declared war against Great Britain and Spain. Southerners became alarmed when the French Caribbean colony of Saint Domingue broke out in revolt, the slaves aided by the British. Northern merchants feared for their prosperity because it rested on good relations with Great Britain, where the United States sent most of its exports.

While the alliance between France and the United States (created in 1778) remained in effect, Washington knew his country was not prepared, militarily or politically, to take sides in a European war. He issued a proclamation of neutrality on April 22, 1793. At that time, the French government had sent Edmond Genet as minister to the United States. Citizen Genet, as he was known, behaved in a decidedly undiplomatic manner. Landing in Charleston, he began recruiting volunteers to fight for France against Britain and Spain. He appointed Revolutionary War hero George Rogers Clark a general, and Clark advertised for troops and support for a campaign against the Spanish at New Orleans. The effort failed for lack of money, but Genet was successful in recruiting privateers. Nearly a thousand men responded, and American ships flying the French flag captured more than eighty British ships.

**Problems with Great Britain.** Washington was appalled by the French violations of American neutrality. The British reacted by seizing American merchant ships in the West Indies and abducting American sailors, forcibly enlisting them in the British navy. This practice, known as **impressment,** angered most Americans. The British claim that it was just apprehending its own deserters rang hollow amid reports of U.S. sailors suffering violations of their rights.

Great Britain rescinded its Orders in Council, which justified the seizure of American ships, and Washington used this opportunity to seek a diplomatic solution. John Jay was sent to London to negotiate a treaty to resolve the outstanding issues between the two countries: the British forts in the Northwest Territory, reparations for the American ships taken under the Orders, compensation for slaves taken during the American Revolution, and an end to trade restrictions in the West Indies. Because the British knew from Alexander Hamilton that Washington was determined not to go to war, Jay had little leverage in the negotiations. Nevertheless, through the **Jay Treaty** (1795), the British finally agreed to withdraw from the Northwest and open the West Indies to American trade, although with limitations on certain goods. The question of reparations for slaves was not addressed. U.S. opposition was strong, but the treaty was probably the best that could be achieved under the circumstances. The Senate ultimately ratified the agreement by one vote.

**Successful negotiations with Spain.** The United States fared better in solving important issues with Spain. With Spain's war against France going badly and rumors of French-recruited Americans planning to

attack New Orleans, the Spanish diplomats became amenable to negotiations. Washington sent Thomas Pinckney, then serving as U.S.
minister to Great Britain, to Spain. Pinckney arrived in late June 1795
to find Spanish officials even more receptive than he had anticipated.
Spain recognized the thirty-first parallel as the southern boundary of
the United States, and removed its troops from all territory north of
the line. Americans were granted free use of the Mississippi River to
its mouth and the privilege of deposit (temporary storage) at New Orleans for three years, with an option to renew. The privilege enabled
Americans to avoid customs duties. Commercial privileges in Spain
were also granted to the United States. All these terms were formalized with the signing of the **Treaty of San Lorenzo,** also called
**Pinckney's Treaty,** on October 27, 1795.

## Ideological Challenges

The partial victory of the Jay Treaty and the triumph of Pinckney's
Treaty vindicated Washington's policy of neutrality. These diplomatic achievements, however, did not solve the dilemma of a politically
divided nation. Jefferson and Hamilton, having resigned their posts,
were replaced by less able men. Washington decided that two terms
as president were enough. In his farewell message to Congress in
1797, he condemned the formation of political parties and warned
against entangling alliances with other nations, urging the United
States to stay out of Europe's quarrels. His isolationist remarks influenced American foreign policy for more than a century.

**The election of 1796.** Despite Washington's condemnation of the
formation of political parties, the Federalists and Republicans had developed into full-blown rivals by 1796. Although the Federalists dominated Congress and the presidency, the Republicans grew in strength,
recruiting support from Irish immigrants and French refugees from
Saint Domingue. John Adams, vice president under Washington, was
the Federalist candidate for president; Thomas Pinckney ran for vice

president. Thomas Jefferson was the Republican presidential candidate with Aaron Burr for vice president. The popular vote for this election was not recorded—nor would votes be recorded until 1824.

The process of selecting a president under the Constitution did not provide for partisan elections. When the Electoral College votes were counted, Adams had seventy-one, Jefferson sixty-eight, Pinckney fifty-nine, and Burr thirty. Because the individual with the second highest total in the Electoral College became vice president, Adams had to serve out his presidency with Jefferson, the opposition leader, as his vice president. This glitch was not remedied until the Twelfth Amendment was ratified in 1804, requiring the electors to vote separately for president and vice president. The problem caused mischief again in the election of 1800.

During his term, Adams had to deal with a politically divided nation and opposition from his own political party. There was still considerable support for France, but Jefferson's defeat in the 1796 election prompted French aggression against American ships. More than three hundred merchant ships were seized by the French navy. In this hostile atmosphere, Adams sought to continue Washington's neutrality policy and avoid war with France.

**The XYZ Affair.** The American peace commission, which arrived in Paris in 1797, ran into difficulties almost immediately. Charles de Talleyrand, the French foreign minister, refused to meet with them. He referred the members to three unnamed agents who suggested that negotiations could begin as soon as Talleyrand received $250,000 and France obtained a $12 million loan. When the commission submitted its report to Adams, the letters X, Y, and Z were used to identify the French agents.

Congress responded to this outrage against American diplomatic efforts by voting to arm fifty-four ships to protect American commerce. Between 1798 and 1800, U.S. and French ships fought an undeclared war in the Caribbean, with American ships capturing ninety-three French vessels and the French just one American ship. The Federalists also expanded the regular army to a force of ten thousand men, even though it was highly doubtful that a land war with

France would take place. Republicans feared the use of the army against them should a civil war break out, while the Federalists considered civil war a possibility for which to prepare.

**The Alien and Sedition Acts.** Using the possibility of a war with France as an excuse, the Federalist-dominated Congress passed a set of laws allegedly to protect national security but really directed toward silencing political opposition. Taken together, the laws were called the **Alien and Sedition Acts** (1798). Three of the laws affected noncitizens, but the fourth applied to U.S. citizens and provoked a tremendous outcry of protest.

The **Alien Enemies Act** authorized the president to expel aliens considered likely to commit acts of espionage or sabotage. It remained unenforced until the War of 1812. The **Alien Friends Act** (which expired in June 1800), empowered the president to expel any foreigners considered dangerous to the nation. No proof of wrongdoing was necessary. Republicans claimed the real intent of the law was to silence any immigrants who opposed Federalist policies. Republicans also protested against passage of the **Naturalization Act,** which extended the naturalization requirement for U.S. citizenship from five to fourteen years, the last five of which required residence in the same state. The law was clearly meant to prevent immigrants, especially the Irish, from voting because they were likely to support the Republicans.

The **Sedition Act** made it a crime to "combine or conspire" to oppose any policy of the United States or to intimidate public officials. It was also illegal to "write, print, utter, or publish" anything deemed false or scandalous about the government of the United States, including Congress or the president—a clear violation of the First Amendment. Under the law, which the Federalists used to suppress opposition to their policies, healthy political dissent was lumped with inciting rebellion. On the possibility that they might lose the election of 1800, the Federalists set an 1801 expiration date for the Sedition Act so it could not be used against them.

Republican newspaper editors became the main target of the Sedition Act. Ten editors and writers went to prison on charges of sedition, among them Vermont Congressman Matthew Lyon. Besides writing an article criticizing Adams, Lyon had spit in a Federalist's eye and wrestled him to the floor—not the best example of political martyrdom—but the Republicans made the most of his imprisonment.

**The Kentucky and Virginia Resolutions.** Republicans protested against the repressive Alien and Sedition Acts. Writing anonymously, Jefferson and Madison created philosophical justifications for states to oppose federal laws they believed unconstitutional. Jefferson wrote the Kentucky Resolutions, and Madison wrote the Virginia Resolutions; both were endorsed by the respective states in 1798. The manifestos claimed that state legislatures had the right to protect the liberties of their citizens by taking a stand against unconstitutional federal laws; this view was called the **doctrine of interposition.** Another concept, **nullification,** was the right of states to cancel, or nullify, federal laws they found unacceptable. None of the other states endorsed the Kentucky or Virginia Resolutions, which took the position that federal law was *not* the supreme law of the land. However, the philosophical underpinnings of these resolutions would surface again in the nullification controversy of the 1830s and the efforts of John C. Calhoun to justify states' rights.

**The election of 1800.** In 1800, Jefferson again ran for president with Aaron Burr as the vice-presidential candidate. John Adams was the logical candidate for the Federalists, but his party had split into two factions. The "High Federalists" considered Alexander Hamilton to be their leader, and they favored such extreme measures as declaring war on France as a ploy to win the election. Adams opposed such ideas and took a moderate position toward France, supporting negotiation.

Voters wanted to avoid war with France and blamed the Federalists for drastically increasing taxes to support an army that had no war to fight. Federalist strength plummeted just two years after the triumph of the 1798 congressional elections. United against the Federalists, the Republicans cast an equal number of electoral votes (seventy-three) for Jefferson and Burr, with Adams and Charles Pinckney receiving sixty-five and sixty-four votes, respectively. The tie threw the election into the Federalist-controlled House of Representatives. When Burr decided to challenge his running mate, Alexander Hamilton used his considerable influence to back Jefferson, who was elected on the thirty-sixth ballot.

The election of 1800 is viewed as a major watershed in American politics, marking the beginning of Jeffersonian democracy. However, in 1800, white men who did not own property could not vote, and women had no direct voice in politics at all. Native Americans were clearly seen as an impediment to American expansion, and their lands and rights were shrinking before the advance of the frontier. For African Americans, the years following the American Revolution at first seemed positive. Several northern states abolished slavery, and it was prohibited in the Northwest Territory. But the Constitution accepted slavery, and the Fugitive Slave Law of 1793 denied even free blacks the protections in the Bill of Rights. The success of cotton as a cash crop in the southern states, provided in part by the efficiency of the cotton gin, increased the demand for slave labor. Jefferson had become president, but it made little or no difference to the conditions of blacks, slave or free, Native Americans, or women.

The inauguration of Thomas Jefferson as the nation's third president marked a turning point in American politics. For the next two dozen years, Republican leadership guided the nation through peace and war. While the Federalists faded as a political force, their ideology continued to influence the country for decades in the decisions handed down by the Supreme Court. Indeed, the judiciary finally attained coequal status as one of the branches of government after 1800.

The period of Republican ascendancy witnessed the doubling of the size of the country through the Louisiana Purchase (1803) and the addition of eight states (1803–21). The admission of Maine and Missouri raised the expansion of slavery into a national issue and set the stage for the sectional debates that raged in the decades before the Civil War.

**Jefferson's first term.** Jefferson had been alarmed by the growth of the national debt under Federalist rule. Albert Gallatin, his secretary of the treasury, agreed that the debt created high taxes that creditors manipulated to their own advantage. Gallatin promised to eliminate the national debt in sixteen years by reducing both military expenditures and the size of government. The Republicans also repealed internal taxes, including the hated excise on whiskey. These policies bore fruit; early in the administration, both military and other governmental spending dropped, and debt declined modestly.

Despite his strict constructionist views, Jefferson did not dismantle important elements of the Federalist program. He saw no need, for example, to abolish the Bank of the United States; it was working well. Nor did Jefferson systematically replace Federalist officeholders with Republicans; rather, he filled vacancies with his supporters as Federalists resigned or died. A number of Federalists even served in his cabinet. In making judicial appointments, however, Jefferson took the upper hand.

*Marbury* v. *Madison* **and judicial review.** In an effort to maintain influence at the national level, the Federalist-controlled Congress passed the **Judiciary Act of 1801** at the end of February, just before Jefferson took office. The legislation reduced the number of justices on the Supreme Court from six to five, and also created sixteen federal judgeships, which President Adams quickly filled with Federalists. No Republicans were on the federal bench at the time, and Jefferson would have virtually no opportunity to appoint any during his term in office. The appointing of "midnight judges" on Adams's last day in office prompted Jefferson to challenge the Judiciary Act.

Secretary of State James Madison refused to issue William Marbury his commission to serve as justice of the peace in the District of Columbia. Marbury then petitioned the Supreme Court to get his judgeship. Chief Justice John Marshall, a Federalist who had recently been appointed to the Supreme Court, rejected Marbury's plea on the grounds that the Judiciary Act of 1789 had incorrectly given the Supreme Court the power to take such action. Meanwhile, Congress repealed the Judiciary Act of 1801.

At first impression, it might seem that by rejecting Marbury's claim, Marshall was not acting in the interest of a fellow Federalist. Marshall, however, had a greater goal in mind. By overturning part of a congressional law, he established the Supreme Court's power of **judicial review**—the power to declare federal laws invalid if they violated the Constitution. Until *Marbury* v. *Madison* (1803), the Supreme Court had not been considered an especially important branch of the federal government. In fact, Marshall was the fourth chief justice to serve in a dozen years. The decision established the Court as a major force in American politics.

**The Barbary pirates.** American merchant ships entering the Mediterranean Sea were subject to seizure by pirates operating out of Tripoli, Algiers, Tunis, and Morocco. The United States had paid tribute to the rulers of the North African states since the 1790s. Although maintaining peace was a cornerstone of Republican foreign policy, Jefferson took action when the pasha of Tripoli made extraordinary demands for payment and declared war on the United States (1801).

The conflict, which led to an American naval blockade and bombardment of Tripoli as well as a land assault by marines, ended in 1805 when a new treaty was signed and the United States agreed to pay a ransom for its captured soldiers and sailors. During the same time, a threat much closer to home was also resolved by paying cash.

**The Louisiana Purchase.** Napoleon Bonaparte, who came to power in France in 1799, dreamed of reestablishing the French empire in North America. In the following year, he negotiated a secret treaty, the **Treaty of San Ildefonso,** with Spanish King Charles IV, which returned the Louisiana Territory, lost at the end of the Seven Years' War, to France. But the agreement did not remain secret for long.

This turn of events just a few years after the successful Pinckney Treaty had opened the Mississippi River and port of New Orleans to American traffic justifiably alarmed Jefferson. His concern was reinforced when a Spanish official in New Orleans forbade the deposit of American produce there for transshipment to other countries, an action many Americans incorrectly believed was ordered by Napoleon. Jefferson feared that France might leave the Mediterranean to British influence in return for a new opportunity on the North American continent. U.S. expansion might be blocked by France to the west and by British Canada to the north.

In 1803, Jefferson sent James Monroe to join Robert Livingston, the American minister in Paris, to negotiate the purchase of New Orleans and West Florida. By this time, Napoleon had given up his plans for a colonial empire. His trying to restore French rule after a slave revolt in Saint Domingue (Haiti) cost him a great deal in both money and men, his troops having been decimated by tropical diseases. The two American representatives were therefore surprised to find the French government willing to sell all of Louisiana—280,000 square miles between the Mississippi River and the Rocky Mountains—for a paltry $15 million. Jefferson was unsure whether the United States could legally buy the Louisiana territory because the Constitution said nothing about purchasing land. He considered proposing a constitutional amendment but dropped the idea because it might take too much time, and the opportunity could vanish. The bargain was too good to pass up. Jefferson approved the purchase, the Senate ratified it, and the United States abruptly doubled in size.

**The Lewis and Clark expedition.** The Louisiana Purchase was then unknown; neither France nor Spain had mapped its rivers, mountains, or plains, and the important sources of the Mississippi and Missouri rivers and their tributaries were still a mystery. Jefferson quickly made plans for its exploration, appointing his secretary, Captain Meriwether Lewis, to head the expedition. Lewis asked his friend Lieutenant William Clark to serve as coleader. In the spring of 1804, the fifty-man Corps of Discovery left St. Louis, heading up the Missouri River. Although military men, Lewis and Clark had received crash courses in botany, zoology, and astronomy, enabling them to carefully collect plant and animal specimens and map the rivers. In addition, every literate man on the expedition was ordered to keep a diary. The expedition spent the first winter among the hospitable Mandan on the Upper Missouri River and then headed west for the Pacific coast in the spring of 1805. Accompanying them were a French fur trader, Toussaint Charbonneau, as guide and interpreter; his wife, a Shoshone Indian named Sacajawea; and their infant son. The presence of the baby and a fortuitous meeting with Shoshone tribesmen reinforced Lewis and Clark's claim that they came in peace. They distributed medallions to the tribal chiefs along with other gifts and pledged their friendship.

On reaching the Pacific in November 1805, the expedition returned eastward. The journals kept by Lewis and Clark and other members of the expedition provided a wealth of information about the geography, the plant and animal life, and the customs of native tribes in the trans-Mississippi west. In addition to stimulating later settlement and trade in the region, the expedition reinforced the American claim to the Oregon Country that was first made by Lieutenant Robert Gray, who came upon the Columbia River in 1792.

Jefferson authorized other expeditions as well. He sent Lieutenant Zebulon Pike to map the source of the Mississippi River. Pike's map was later proved incorrect, however, due mainly to the complexity of the rivers and lakes at the headwaters. Pike also headed west to explore the area between the Arkansas and Red rivers, but he became lost and was taken into custody by Spanish soldiers on the Rio Grande. Although his maps and papers were confiscated, Pike remembered enough to reconstruct a good deal of his records after he was released.

## Maintaining Neutrality under Jefferson and Madison

Jefferson had no problem trouncing his Federalist opponent in 1804. Obtaining the Louisiana Purchase and accomplishing a reduction of the national debt assured him of an overwhelming electoral victory.

**A troubled second term.** The Republicans' elation at the results of the election did not last long. A disaffected Aaron Burr, whose political career ended when he killed Alexander Hamilton in a duel, became involved in a plot either to create an independent nation in the Louisiana-Mississippi-West Florida region or invade Mexico. Historians remain unsure. Burr was indicted in two states for Hamilton's death, and in early 1807, he was arrested on Jefferson's order and charged with treason. His trial before Chief Justice John Marshall ended in an acquittal because Marshall defined treason under the Constitution very narrowly. The Burr case is interesting from another constitutional perspective: Jefferson refused to turn over documents or appear in court to testify based on a claim of executive privilege.

With the Federalist party rapidly declining, Jefferson had to meet the challenge of growing factionalism within his own party. One group, known as the Quids, criticized the president for compromising Republican ideology. John Randolph, the Quid leader, refused to accept the idea that a political party on taking power might have to view things differently than when it was in opposition to the party in office. For example, Jefferson endured Randolph's attacks for agreeing to a compromise on the Yazoo land fraud, a Georgia-area land speculation scheme in which innocent buyers of fraudulently purchased land would have lost their investments. Foreign policy, rather than party or domestic issues, dominated his second term and the administration of his successor, James Madison.

**War between France and Great Britain.** The renewed fighting between Great Britain and France (1803) severely tested American neutrality. The situation became even more difficult when the British navy under Lord Nelson defeated the French fleet at the Battle of Trafalgar in 1805 and gained control of the seas. American merchants had been profiting from the war by shipping sugar and coffee brought from French and Spanish colonies in the Caribbean to Europe. Great Britain protested because the prices it was getting for its West Indies products were declining. Noting that French ports visited by neutral U.S. merchant ships (to preserve the French merchant marine from Great Britain) would have been closed to the United States in peacetime (allowing only French deliveries), Britain invoked the Rule of 1756, stating that such ports should not be open during war to neutral replacements. American traders got around the rule by taking French and Spanish products to American ports, unloading them, and then reloading them for European ports as "American" exports.

By 1805, Britain had had enough of such deceptions, and through a series of trade decrees began a blockade of French-controlled European ports. The British as well as the French ignored U.S. neutrality claims and seized American merchant ships. Great Britain resumed the policy of impressment, taking alleged British navy deserters off American vessels and returning them to British service. The life of an American sailor was hard but nothing like that in the Royal Navy with its harsh discipline and low pay. Many British deserters had become American citizens, but this did not stop British officials from impressing them, nor did the British hesitate in taking U.S.-born citizens, who could even prove their American birth. Between 1807 and 1812, the Royal Navy impressed some six thousand American seamen.

In June 1807, the British warship *Leopard* attacked the *Chesapeake,* an American navy frigate, and four alleged deserters were removed. Prior impressment actions had involved merchant ships; this one, however, involved a U.S. navy ship. Amid the public's cry for war against Britain, Jefferson turned to economic pressure to resolve the crisis.

**The Embargo Act.** Jefferson's solution to the problems with Great Britain and France was to deny both countries American goods. In December 1807, Congress passed the **Embargo Act,** which stopped exports and prohibited the departure of merchant ships for foreign ports. The act also effectively ended imports because foreign ships would not bring products to the United States if they had to leave without cargo. The British got around the Embargo Act by developing trade connections in South America, while in the United States, thousands of sailors were thrown out of work, merchants declared bankruptcy, and southern and western farmers had no outlet for their crops.

At the time, the Embargo Act was generally viewed as a failure. While the economic costs to Americans were high, trade did continue. Enforcement was lax, and American captains used a loophole in the law to claim that they had legally sailed into European ports only after being "blown off course" by adverse winds; there were a suspiciously great many instances of bad weather between 1807 and 1809. The Embargo Act did, however, result in an increase in manufacturing. The number of cotton mills in the United States, for example, increased from fifteen to eighty-seven in just two years, and other domestic industries took root to replace foreign imports.

The mood of the country in 1808 encouraged Jefferson not to seek a third term. Despite the nation's unhappiness over the embargo, Republican James Madison was elected president and the Republicans kept control of both houses of Congress. The Embargo Act was repealed on March 1, 1809, just before Madison took office.

**Madison and neutrality.** Madison was just as committed as Jefferson to staying out of the European war, and he continued to rely on economic pressure. The **Non-Intercourse Act** of 1809 replaced the

Embargo Act. The logic behind the law was that the United States would open its ports to all nations *except* Britain and France. If either of those two nations stopped violating American neutrality rights, the United States would reestablish commercial ties. Britain and France ignored the Non-Intercourse Act, and other seafaring nations had no desire to confront the Royal Navy. Many American merchants simply found ways to evade the law. Congress tried another tack in May 1810 with **Macon's Bill No. 2.** This time, the United States would trade with Britain and France, in spite of their neutrality violations. Should one of them end their restrictions on neutral shipping, the United States would stop trading with the other. A cynical Napoleon responded by promising to end French restrictions, and Congress proclaimed non-intercourse against Britain in February 1811, but France continued to seize American ships.

**Problems in the west.** While Madison and Congress grappled with the neutrality issue, Native Americans renewed their objections to American settlement north of the Ohio River. Tribes were still being coerced into giving away or selling their land. Through the Treaty of Fort Wayne (1809), the Delaware and Miami gave up much of the central and western parts of the new Indiana Territory for only ten thousand dollars.

Two Shawnee leaders, Tecumseh, a brilliant chief, and his half-brother Tenskwatawa, known as the Prophet, took a stand against further encroachment by settlers. While Tecumseh did receive aid from the British in Canada, he was less their pawn than a man who clearly saw what alcoholism, disease, and loss of land were doing to his people. Tenskwatawa was a recovered alcoholic who urged Indians to reaffirm their traditional values and culture. William Henry Harrison, the governor of the Indiana Territory, perceived in Tecumseh and the Prophet a dangerous combination of military and religious appeal. In September 1811, Harrison set out with about one thousand men to attack Tecumseh's stronghold at Prophetstown on the Tippecanoe River. The Shawnee struck first, but Harrison was able to beat them back and claim a major victory. Tecumseh was away from the village trying to recruit tribes to join the confederacy, and Tenskwatawa fled.

The Battle of Tippecanoe, as Harrison preferred to call the engagement, clearly did not resolve the conflict with the Indians on the frontier. It did, however, intensify anti-British feeling in the Northwest.

Western senators and congressmen urged a more aggressive policy against Great Britain. Henry Clay of Kentucky became the leader of a faction in Congress called the **War Hawks,** which demanded an invasion of Canada and the expulsion of Spain from Florida. The War Hawks feared that the British in Canada were once again intriguing with the Indians, a concern that had provoked Harrison's move against Tecumseh.

**Voting for war.** On June 1, 1812, President Madison sent a war message to Congress. Frustrated at the failure of the neutrality measures and pressured by the War Hawks, Madison felt he had no choice. Ironically, Great Britain repealed its Orders in Council on June 23, 1812, relaxing its trade restrictions in the face of an economic depression. American leaders ignored this belated attempt at compromise, however. Few Republicans wanted war, but long-standing grievances and insults could no longer be tolerated. Madison's war message cited impressment, violation of neutral rights, Indian aggression, and British meddling in American trade as causes for war. The vote proceeded along party lines, the majority of Republicans voting for war and a Federalist minority voting against it. A somewhat divided United States thus fought Great Britain for a second time.

## The War of 1812

Although the dispute leading to the War of 1812 was over freedom of the seas, the war itself was fought chiefly on land. Madison believed that the motive behind British policy had been to eliminate the United States as a maritime trading rival, while the British, occupied with fighting France in a battle for survival, considered the war with the United States a sideshow, at least initially.

**The Canadian campaign.** For the United States, the most obvious British target was Canada. Its population was small, many Canadians were actually Americans by birth, and a quick victory there would stop British plans to ruin American trade. The military facts painted a different picture, however. Thousands of Native Americans in the northwestern territories sided with the British when the war began, bolstering their strength, while the small U.S. army was composed of poorly trained state militiamen led by elderly and incompetent generals.

In July 1812, an American army led by General William Hull moved from Detroit into Canada. Almost immediately the Shawnee cut his supply lines, forcing him back to Detroit. Although Hull commanded two thousand men, he surrendered to a considerably smaller British and Native American force. Other embarrassments followed as the United States suffered defeat at Queenston Heights in western New York, and the militia under General Henry Dearborn refused to march to Montreal from northeastern New York.

The United States fared better on Lake Erie in 1813. The Royal Navy could not reach the lake from the St. Lawrence River, so both the British and Americans raced to build ships on opposite sides of the lake. On September 10, 1813, the small American fleet under Oliver Hazard Perry defeated the British in the Battle of Lake Erie. "We have met the enemy, and they are ours," he reported, a victory statement that became legendary.

Less than three weeks later, on October 5, William Henry Harrison (a general by then) defeated a combined British and Native American force at the Battle of the Thames. Tecumseh was killed in this battle, ending Native Americans' hopes for a coalition that could stand against the advance of U.S. settlement. Despite these victories, U.S. efforts to capture Canada ended in stalemate.

**The British land offensive.** In April 1814, Napoleon abdicated the French throne and went into exile on the island of Elba, allowing Great Britain to devote its full attention to the war in the United States. The British sent a fleet to Chesapeake Bay and landed an army at Bladensburg, Maryland, on August 24, 1814. The American militia troops fled before the British, who then headed for the U.S. capital. Madison fled Washington, D.C., along with the militia, while his wife Dolley rescued silverware, a bed, and a painting of Washington before leaving the presidential home at the last minute. The British burned the mansion and other public buildings, partly in retaliation for an American act of arson at the Canadian capital of York (now Toronto) during the previous year.

Continuing north in Chesapeake Bay, the British fleet intended to capture Baltimore after first taking Fort McHenry. The British bombarded the fort all through the night of September 13. Francis Scott Key, an American attorney who had boarded a British ship to negotiate the release of a civilian prisoner, watched the battle rage. At dawn, the British broke off the attack, unable to take the fort. Key scribbled down a poem about the event, which became the national anthem "The Star-Spangled Banner."

Almost simultaneously, a British naval force under General Sir George Prevost advanced from Canada along Lake Champlain. They met the Americans under Commander Thomas Macdonough at Plattsburgh, New York, on September 11. Macdonough won a decisive victory, forcing Prevost to retreat to Canada. Earlier American victories near Niagara had halted a British offensive there.

The British also planned a major sea and land offensive at New Orleans. The plan stemmed from victories by Andrew Jackson's army against the Creek Indians in Florida in March 1814 and the subsequent capture of the Spanish fort at Pensacola in November, denying its use as a base to the British. A British force of more than seven thousand men landed near New Orleans in December with the goal of seizing Mississippi. Jackson's defensive strategy was excellent. By placing his outnumbered troops behind earthworks and cotton bales, he was able to cut down more than two thousand British soldiers in short order during their engagement on January 8, 1815. The Battle of New Orleans was seen as the victory that ended the war. In fact, a peace treaty had been signed several weeks earlier. A battle that never would have been fought if international communications had been faster made Andrew Jackson a national hero.

**Ending the war.** At about the same time the British were besieging Fort McHenry, American and British commissioners were meeting at Ghent, Belgium, to work out an agreement to end the war. With Napoleon out of the picture (he did not escape from Elba until March 1815), the British had little reason for continuing the war. While the British initially called for the surrender of some American territory, news of their loss in the Battle of Plattsburgh made them more conciliatory. The American commissioners, led by John Quincy Adams, hammered out the details of the peace settlement. Essentially, the treaty simply ended the conflict. It said nothing about the impressment of American sailors, freedom of the seas, or neutral rights, all of which had led to the war. The commissioners signed the Treaty of Ghent on December 24, 1814, in time to celebrate Christmas Eve.

**A Federalist error.** The election of 1812 had seen a Federalist comeback in national politics. Although Madison won reelection against DeWitt Clinton, the electoral vote was the closest since 1800: 128 to 89. During the war, New England had become a Federalist stronghold. Federalists there had opposed the Louisiana Purchase for its potential threat to New England's economic importance. New England's commerce had been wrecked by the Embargo Act, and some unhappy New Englanders called the war "Mr. Madison's War."

Despite the complaints, New Englanders had profited from the war, sending grain to feed the British army and building factories with war profits. New England banks refused to accept paper money and consequently amassed huge amounts of silver and gold, causing a scarcity of specie (hard money) in the rest of the United States.

New England's opposition to the war prompted the Federalists to call a special convention in Hartford, Connecticut, on December 15, 1814, where they proposed a series of constitutional amendments that would have severely limited the power of the national government. Their resolutions were badly timed, for hardly had they announced their proposals when news came that the war was over, making the Federalist resolutions seem unpatriotic at best and treasonable at worst. At the next presidential election (1816), voter rejection of the Federalist party was nearly complete. James Monroe, yet another Virginia Republican, defeated Rufus King by 183 electoral votes to 34. The Federalist party was through in national politics.

## A Spirit of Nationalism

Monroe's presidency brought one-party rule to the United States, but the unanimity was more apparent than real. Although the Republicans controlled the presidency and Congress, some Republican leaders were developing their own political program. Henry Clay endorsed what he called an **American System,** which included tariff protection for new industries, federal support for internal improvements such as roads and bridges, and renewal of the national bank, ideas not far removed from what Federalists advocated. Many Republicans agreed with Clay. Congress approved the Second Bank of the United States in 1816 for a twenty-year period and passed a moderate tariff in the same year.

Internal improvements were another matter. Federal spending on roads began under Jefferson when Congress agreed to fund the construction of the **National Road** from the Atlantic coast into Ohio, but Republicans were never comfortable with the idea. Although roads and canals could be justified as "necessary and proper" to carry out such legitimate functions of the federal government as the promotion of commerce, they believed these programs really were the responsibility of the states, absent a constitutional amendment. Madison used this argument in vetoing a bill that would have appropriated money for internal improvements.

**The Era of Good Feelings.** With the embargo in the past and the country at peace, a Boston newspaper editor called the postwar period the "Era of Good Feelings." Monroe sought reconciliation of political differences, so the nickname of the era also applied to his administration. In 1820, Monroe won reelection handily by 231 votes to 1; the sole dissenting elector voted for John Quincy Adams, who ran as an Independent Republican.

Even as political leaders spoke in nationalist terms, new issues surfaced to create new political divisions. John Marshall's Supreme Court handed down decisions that clearly favored a strong national government, even though the party representing that view, the Federalist, was defunct. In the *Dartmouth College* case (1819), the Court ruled that charters granted by the states to private organizations were contracts protected under the contract clause of the Constitution, and state legislatures had no right to impair these contracts. The decision in *McCulloch* v. *Maryland* (1819), which denied the states the power to tax a federal agency (in this case the Second Bank of the United States), recognized that while the powers of the federal government were limited, the government was "supreme within its sphere of action."

**New states and a new crisis.** Since 1812, five states had been added to the Union, bringing the total to twenty-two: Louisiana (1812), Indiana (1816), Mississippi (1817), Illinois (1818), and Alabama (1819). In February 1819, Missouri Territory applied for statehood, but its proposed constitution permitted slavery, and at this point, eleven of the twenty-two states were "free" and eleven were "slave" states. Admitting Missouri would thus upset the existing balance. After considerable debate, a compromise credited to Henry Clay's efforts was reached. Maine, which was cleaved from Massachusetts, was admitted as a free state, followed by Missouri's admission as a slave state; the balance between free and slave states was thus preserved by the **Missouri Compromise.** Southerners agreed that slavery would not be permitted north of the 36°30′ line in the Louisiana Purchase. The next six territories to become states would continue the fragile balancing act.

**Monroe's foreign policy.** Secretary of State John Quincy Adams successfully concluded the **Transcontinental Treaty** (also called the **Adams-Onís Treaty**) with Spain, in which Spain gave up its unprofitable and troublesome Florida colony in return for $5 million and a clear boundary line running from the Sabine River between Spanish Texas and Louisiana across to the Pacific Ocean.

Adams followed this successful negotiation with a policy statement regarding the new Latin American republics. Approached by the British to join an alliance supporting Latin American independence, Adams proposed instead to create a policy that would inform Europe that the Western Hemisphere was no longer open to colonization and that any such attempt would be viewed by the United States as an unfriendly act. In return, the United States pledged not to get involved in European problems. Because these ideas were written into Monroe's annual message to Congress, the policy eventually became known as the **Monroe Doctrine.**

The Era of Good Feelings did not survive Monroe's two terms as president. By 1824, nationalism was being replaced by the growth of **sectionalism,** or the sense of one's place being in a portion of the nation rather than in the nation as a whole. Thus, even as developments in transportation and communication worked to unite the nation, political differences threatened to pull it apart.

The period between the end of the War of 1812 and the Civil War was a time of swift improvement in transportation, rapid growth of factories, and significant development of new technology to increase agricultural production. Americans moved with relative ease into new regions and soon produced an agricultural surplus that changed them from subsistence farmers into commercial producers. Manufacturing became an increasingly important sector of the economy and set the stage for rapid industrialization in the late nineteenth century. The economic and technological developments brought important changes to American society.

## Improvements in Transportation

The growth and expansion of the United States in the decades before the Civil War were closely tied to improvements in the nation's transportation system. As farmers shifted from growing just enough to sustain their families (**subsistence agriculture**) to producing crops for sale (**commercial agriculture**), demand grew for cheaper and faster ways to get goods to market. Steamboats made river ports important commercial points for entire regions; canals had a similar impact in the Northeast and the Midwest, particularly near the Great Lakes. Railroads, which carried mostly passengers at first, became essential for moving both farm products and manufactured goods by 1860.

**Inland waterways.** As settlers moved into the trans-Appalachian region, they found the river systems crucial for exporting products to distant markets. Many streams were navigable, and they led to larger rivers such as the Tennessee and Cumberland, which in turn fed into the Ohio, which merged with the Mississippi River and flowed past the port of New Orleans. With roads unable to handle bulk traffic, farmers in Tennessee, Kentucky, western Pennsylvania, and the Ohio Valley could take their harvest to an eastern city such as New York by riding down river to New Orleans and then taking a ship around Florida. The Mississippi River was thus a major means of transporting agricultural products from the Old Northwest to the East Coast, and its free navigation was vital to American interests.

The simplest means of river transport were rafts, but they were unstable, and rapids especially posed a serious danger. Flatboats could carry more cargo, providing an interior space for the storage of products and supplies. Real improvement, however, came with the **keelboat.** Its design made it more controllable, and a small crew using poles could propel a keelboat downstream at a fairly rapid rate. As many as one thousand keelboats a year headed down trans-Appalachian tributaries and rivers to New Orleans in the early 1800s. Unfortunately, rafts, flatboats, and keelboats had one major disadvantage—they could make only a one-way trip. After arriving in New Orleans, the rafts and flatboats were broken up and sold for wood. Poling upriver in a keelboat was possible, but a trip from New Orleans to Louisville, Kentucky, could take as long as four months, so return trips were usually over land. The Natchez Trace led travelers from north of New Orleans to Nashville. A map from the time would have shown the barest outline of roads radiating from New Orleans and Mobile, a city located about one hundred miles to the east. To call these byways "roads" is misleading though; they were often little more than trails, unsuitable for wagons in many places.

Two-way river transportation came with the invention of the **steamboat,** or **riverboat.** A number of inventors had attempted to use steam engines to power boats, but the most successful design was created by Robert Fulton in 1807 and used on the *Clermont.* Fulton demonstrated the watercraft on the Hudson River and won a monopoly from the New York legislature to form a steamboat ferrying service between New York and New Jersey. The monopoly was broken in 1824 when Marshall's Supreme Court, in *Gibbons* v. *Ogden,* declared that regulation of interstate commerce, a federal power, also applied to navigation.

Steamboat transportation on trans-Appalachian rivers met with great enthusiasm. Steamboats quickly succeeded rafts, flatboats, and keelboats as the main vehicle for river travel. (Keelboats continued to be used in the upper reaches of tributary streams.) As steamboats evolved, they were built with shallower drafts, so they could operate in as little as three feet of water. Enormous above water, they could carry hundreds of tons of freight and dozens of passengers. Towns along the rivers benefited greatly from the economic exchange provided by steamboats. Cincinnati, Ohio, for example, grew from a small settlement in 1770 to the sixth largest city in the country in 1840 on the strength of river travel. A common scene was the loading and unloading of furniture, farm machinery, bales of cotton, and bulk agricultural products at the town wharf.

**The canal craze.** After the War of 1812, DeWitt Clinton of New York boldly suggested that a canal be constructed from Lake Erie to Albany (363 miles) using the Mohawk River and then the Hudson River to connect with New York City. Such a project had no precedent in the United States. Clinton obtained a subsidy from the New York legislature and began construction on July 4, 1817. Completed in 1825, the **Erie Canal** was an instant success, bringing prosperity and additional settlement to its western terminus at Buffalo and helping to make New York City the preeminent American seaport. Philadelphia merchants, jealous of New York's success, pressed for a canal between eastern Pennsylvania and Pittsburgh, but this waterway presented even greater obstacles than the New York project. The 395-mile Pennsylvania Canal required 174 locks—more than double the number on the Erie Canal—and a funicular railway to get cargo over the Allegheny Mountains. Completed in 1834, it carried considerable traffic but never rivaled the Erie Canal in terms of total tonnage or economic impact.

The success of these projects fed a craze for canal construction throughout the Midwest. By 1837, companies had built 750 miles of canals in Ohio alone. Canals linked Toledo to Cincinnati, Evansville to Fort Wayne, and Akron to Cleveland. While financially risky private investments, canals benefited farmers throughout the Ohio Valley and the Great Lakes region by providing a relatively inexpensive means to get their produce to market. Even though the barges that carried lumber, coal, hay, wheat, corn, and oats traveled only two miles an hour (they were towed by mules walking along the banks), the canals greatly reduced shipping costs, time, and distances. They also contributed to a shift in population as cities like Buffalo, Cleveland, Detroit, Chicago, and Milwaukee grew at the expense of such river ports as Louisville.

**Railroads.** Railroad construction began in the United States in 1825; by 1860, more than thirty thousand miles of track had been laid. Originally concentrated in the Northeast, by the eve of the Civil War, lines reached as far west as St. Joseph, Missouri. In the South, railroad building lagged just as much as canal building.

Railroads had several advantages over canals. They required a smaller initial capital investment; offered more direct routes; and provided fast, year-round service (rivers and canals froze in winter). There was little coordination among the different railroads though, which worked against creation of a uniform rail system. Because the companies selected their own track gauge, freight often had to be unloaded at the terminus of one line and reloaded at the start of another line, adding to costs. Despite this shortcoming and their comparatively high maintenance costs, railroads expanded and eventually moved ahead of canals in total tonnage shipped in the late 1840s.

**Roads.** Although road building was the earliest sign of the impending transportation revolution, it was not an important factor in economic development prior to the Civil War. The **Lancaster Turnpike** (1794), which started in Philadelphia, spurred similar private toll roads. Around the same time, the **Wilderness Road** into Kentucky was opened to wagon traffic and figured in the settlement of the lower Ohio River Valley. The **National Road,** a paved highway extending west from Cumberland, Maryland, was financed and maintained through congressional appropriations. It was completed as far as Wheeling on the Ohio River in 1818 and then extended over the next twenty years to Vandalia, Illinois. The federal funding of the National

Road was an exception rather than the norm; throughout the nineteenth century, roads were either the responsibility of local government or were built under charters granted by the states.

With the exception of the important east-west and north-south turnpikes, roads throughout the country were often narrow and unpaved, muddy in wet weather and dusty in dry. Moving freight by road was expensive and slow. Roads between towns were often neglected after the railroad arrived, and only the use of the automobile in the twentieth century created the public demand for a modern highway system.

## Toward a Market Economy

Several factors played a role in the development of the market economy in the United States. Millions of acres of land belonging to Native Americans in the Old Northwest and Southeast were taken over by the federal government. Federal land policy, though often benefiting speculators more than individual homesteaders, certainly encouraged settlement. American agriculture experienced an unprecedented boom from the introduction of new staple crops, such as cotton, and productivity advancements in farm equipment. Although the United States remained overwhelmingly rural, the country experienced significant urban growth between 1815 and 1860.

**Removal of Native Americans.** The economic growth of the United States was achieved to a great degree at the expense of Native Americans. Despite giving up tens of thousands of acres through treaties, the tribes found the demand for land by settlers and speculators insatiable. Even the willingness of Native Americans to acculturate did not relieve the pressure on their land. The Cherokee—one of the "Five Civilized Tribes" along with the Creek, Choctaw, Chickasaw, and Seminole—were farmers and even owned slaves. They developed a written language in which books, tribal laws, and a constitution were published, and they were ready to press the case for their sovereignty in court. Even though the Supreme Court found in *Worcester*

v. *Georgia* (1832) that the Cherokee were entitled to federal protection of their lands against state claims, President Andrew Jackson did not enforce the decision.

Jackson's solution to the land question was to resettle the tribes west of the Mississippi, which Congress authorized through the **Indian Removal Act of 1830.** Within a few years, the Creek, Choctaw, and Chickasaw had given up their lands in Alabama, Arkansas, and Mississippi and were moved to the Indian Territory in what is today Oklahoma. The Cherokee held out until 1838. Of the approximately fifteen thousand Cherokee who took the grueling trek from Georgia to the west, a route that became known as the **Trail of Tears,** a quarter died of disease and exposure. Some tribes resisted relocation. The Sauk and Fox were easily defeated by U.S. troops and militia forces in the **Black Hawk War** (1832), and the Seminoles fought a guerrilla action in Florida for seven years (1835–42). In the end, however, more than 200 million acres of Indian land passed into the control of the United States.

**Federal land policy.** The sale of public lands, which the federal government offered at $2 per acre (for a minimum of 160 acres) with four years to pay, increased quickly after the War of 1812. Land speculators were encouraged by the credit provisions, and they bought up land with the expectation of turning a profit when its value rose. The Panic of 1819 and the economic depression that followed led to legal changes intended to make the direct purchase of land easier for small farmers. The price was cut to $1.25 an acre, and the minimum amount of land that could be purchased was reduced first to eighty acres (1820) and then to forty acres (1832), but payments had to be made in cash, which many settlers did not have. Speculators continued to buy up most of the available land and then loan money to small farmers for the purchase price and farm equipment.

Aside from the terms of purchase, an important issue was the claims of squatters, who had settled and begun to work the land before it was surveyed and auctioned. The **Pre-Emption Act,** enacted as a temporary measure in 1830 and made permanent in 1841, allowed squatters to buy up to 160 acres at the minimum price of $1.25 an acre.

**A boom period for agriculture.** The period from 1815 to 1860 proved a golden age for American agriculture. Demand for American farm products was high, both in the United States and Europe, and agricultural prices and production rose dramatically. A key factor was the increasing importance of cotton. Until the 1790s, cotton was a relatively minor crop because the variety that grew best in the more southerly latitudes contained seeds that were difficult to remove from the cotton boll. In 1793, Eli Whitney of Connecticut learned of the seed problem while visiting friends in South Carolina; he devised a simple machine known as the **cotton gin** to separate the fiber from the seeds. With cotton demand high from the textile industry in Great Britain and soon mills in New England, Whitney's invention led to the expansion of cotton production across Virginia, Alabama, Mississippi, and Louisiana, and into Texas. The **Cotton Kingdom,** as this vast region was called, produced most of the world's cotton supply and more than fifty percent of American exports by 1860.

The cotton boom also revitalized slavery. Despite the end of the foreign slave trade in 1808, more than four times the number of slaves lived in the United States on the eve of the Civil War than on the day Thomas Jefferson took office. Cotton was a labor-intensive crop, causing the demand and price for field hands to skyrocket. Planters in Virginia found it very profitable to sell their surplus slaves farther south.

Cotton was not the only sector of agriculture to benefit from technological innovations. In 1831, Cyrus McCormick invented the mechanical reaper, which harvested considerably more wheat with less labor. John Deere developed a steel plow (1837) that was far more efficient in turning the soil than cast iron and wooden moldboards. The new equipment allowed American farmers to put more land under cultivation and increase production to meet the growing world-wide demand for wheat, corn, and other cereal grains.

**Changing demographics.** During the nineteenth century, the United States became a country on the move. By 1850, almost half of all Americans did not reside in the state where they were born, and the population had made a clear shift to the west. About a third lived west of the Appalachian Mountains, and two million people were already west of the Mississippi River. Rapid urbanization also characterized the pre-Civil War decades. According to the 1850 census, cities (defined as towns with a population of 2500 or more) were home to one in five Americans. Although the nation's largest cities were in the Northeast—New York, Philadelphia, Baltimore, and Boston—the population of St. Louis had already topped one hundred thousand. The midcentury urban growth was caused by improvements in transportation, industrial opportunities, and renewed immigration.

U.S. immigration, which had been sharply curtailed during the Napoleonic wars, began to increase in the 1820s and then rose dramatically—to well over two hundred thousand people a year—in the 1840s and 1850s. Irish Catholics, fleeing the effects of the potato famine that started in 1846, and Germans, seeking either economic opportunity or refuge from the failed liberal revolution of 1848, were the two largest immigrant groups. The Irish were an important part of the labor force that built the canals and railroads, and they tended to remain in the eastern cities. The Germans, on the other hand, moved west and contributed to the growth of St. Louis and Milwaukee. Scandinavians, who had also begun to leave their homelands, established farming communities in Wisconsin and Minnesota.

## The Growth of Manufacturing

American industry grew phenomenally in the first half of the nineteenth century. A series of tariffs enacted by Congress between 1816 and 1828 protected manufacturing, particularly textile milling, from foreign competition. As manufacturing work sites were gradually relocated from the home and small workshop to the factory, the makeup of the labor force changed. The number of artisans and craftsmen declined, and reliance on semiskilled or unskilled workers, including women, to operate machines increased. Just as in agriculture, advances in technology helped boost manufacturing production and increase efficiency. Indeed, the manufacture of such agricultural inventions as the reaper and steel plow became important sectors of the industrial economy.

**Technological innovation.** Machines for spinning cotton into thread were developed in Great Britain in the eighteenth century, and how they were built and operated were closely guarded secrets. Although the British prohibited the emigration of anyone with a knowledge of their design, Samuel Slater arrived in the United States from England with the plans in his head. In 1790, he established the first American cotton mill in Rhode Island.

"Borrowed" technology aside, Americans made their own inventive contributions to industrial development. Eli Whitney, already famous for the cotton gin, developed machine tools capable of producing parts so precisely that they were interchangeable. Interchangeable parts significantly increased industrial efficiency and cut labor costs. Charles Goodyear developed a process known as vulcanization that made natural rubber stronger (1839). The sewing machine was invented by Elias Howe (1846) and improved on a few years later by Isaac Singer.

Perhaps the most significant American invention of the first half of the nineteenth century was Samuel Morse's electric telegraph, which had its first practical application in 1844. Within twenty years, telegraph lines stretched from coast to coast and ushered in a communications revolution. Combined with improvements in printing, the telegraph was a boon to journalism. The number of daily newspapers in the United States soared from eight in 1790 to nearly four hundred in 1860, and many sold for just a penny.

**The factory system.** New England's textile industry led the way in developing new forms of manufacturing. The **factory system** as it evolved in the Northeast had three characteristics—the breakdown of an item's production into phases, the use of machines in all phases of production, and the division of labor. **Division of labor** meant that a worker performed the task required by one phase of the production, no longer creating the entire product from start to finish. In 1813, the first factory in which spinning and weaving were performed by power machinery all under one roof was established in Waltham, Massachusetts. In Lowell, which was planned and built as a model factory town in 1822, young women made up the majority of the workforce at the mills. The women lived in dormitories or boarding houses provided by the company and worked twelve hours a day, six days a week. Although the women were paid much less than the men, even when doing comparable work, their wages were enough to give them a measure of independence that their mothers and grandmothers never enjoyed. The young women were not a permanent labor force in the mills, however. Most of them worked for only a few years and were gradually replaced by immigrants, mainly Irish men, in the 1840s and 1850s.

Textile manufacturing was the leading American industry before the Civil War and was concentrated in the Northeast because the region's rivers provided both water power and transportation. The cloth produced in New England mills was turned into shirts, pants, and other articles of clothing in smaller factories in New York and Philadelphia. Proximity to raw materials influenced industrial development in other parts of the country. For example, Pittsburgh was a center of the iron industry because it was close to both ore and coal fields, while Cincinnati was an early hub for meatpacking in agricultural Ohio.

The development of the factory system produced tensions. Craftsmen were threatened by manufacturing's increasing reliance on machines and cheap labor, so they began to form trade unions and political parties in the 1830s to protect their interests. Although initially antagonistic toward unskilled workers, the craftsmen often discovered that they were on common ground over such issues as hours, wages, and working conditions. The first general strike in the United States took place in Philadelphia in 1835, when artisans joined with coal heavers to support the ten-hour workday. A shorter workday was the principal demand of the early trade unions, and most industries accepted it by the 1860s, with the exception of the New England textile mills.

## Changes in American Society

The economic expansion between 1815 and 1860 was reflected in changes in American society. The changes were most evident in the northern states, where the combined effects of the transportation revolution, urbanization, and the rise of manufacturing were keenly felt. In the northern cities, a small, wealthy percentage of the population controlled a large segment of the economy, while the working poor, whose numbers swelled by large-scale immigration, owned little or nothing. Despite the "rags-to-riches" stories that were popular during the period, wealth remained concentrated in the hands of those who already had it. Opportunities for social mobility were limited, even though personal income was rising. Certainly there were craftsmen who entered the middle class by becoming factory managers or even owners, but many skilled workers found themselves as permanent wage earners with little hope for advancement.

**Women and the family.** The legal position of women in the middle of the nineteenth century was essentially the same as it had been in the colonial period. Although New York gave married women control over their property in 1848, it was the only state to do so. The beginnings of industrialization did change the role that urban, middle-class women in particular played in society. Because of the rise of manufacturing, goods that were once made in the home and that provided an important source of additional income (especially clothing, but also a variety of household items) were produced in factories and sold at low prices. Rather than contributing to the sustenance and economic welfare of their family, women were expected to create a clean and nurturing environment in the home, while their husbands became the sole breadwinners and dealt with the outside world. An important element of this **doctrine of "separate spheres,"** or **"cult of domesticity,"** was the role of mothers in preparing their children for adulthood. Indeed, women were having fewer children on which to lavish their attention. Throughout the first half of the nineteenth century, the birth rate in the United States declined steadily, the drop sharper in the urban upper and middle classes. Although considered an economic asset on the farm, children could be a financial burden in the cities, where clothing, food, and other necessities had to be purchased. Middle-class women controlled the size of their families through abstinence or the birth control methods available at the time, including abortion.

**The status of free blacks.** On the eve of the Civil War, there were just under half a million free blacks in the United States, and slightly more than half lived in the southern states, particularly Maryland, Virginia, and North Carolina. Southern free blacks, or "free persons of color" as they were called, could not vote, hold office, or testify against whites in court. Most were laborers, although some were artisans, farmers, and even slaveowners themselves.

Although slavery had been abolished in the northern states by 1820, the status of free blacks there was not much different from that of free blacks in the southern part of the country. More than ninety percent of the northern blacks were denied voting rights; the notable exception was in New England. New York required blacks to own at least $250 worth of real property to vote, and New Jersey, Pennsylvania, and Connecticut rescinded black suffrage in the early nineteenth century. Segregation was the rule, and blacks were denied civil liberties by both law and tradition. Only Massachusetts allowed blacks to sit on juries, and several Midwestern states prohibited blacks from settling within their boundaries, using laws comparable to those banning free blacks from entering the southern states. In the northern cities, competition between blacks and immigrants—mainly the Irish—for low-wage, unskilled jobs created tensions that erupted in violence. A series of race riots occurred in Philadelphia between 1832 and 1849.

Even though Andrew Jackson was president only from 1829 to 1837, his influence on American politics was pervasive both before and after his time in office. The years from about 1824 to 1840 have been called the "Age of Jacksonian Democracy" and the "Era of the Common Man." By modern standards, however, the United States was far from democratic. Women could not vote and were legally under the control of their husbands; free blacks, if not completely disenfranchised, were considered second-class citizens at best; slavery was growing in the southern states. Moreover, the period witnessed the resettlement of Native Americans west of the Mississippi River and the concentration of wealth in fewer and fewer hands. But changes did occur that broadened participation in politics, and reform movements emerged to address the inequalities in American society.

## The Politics of the Jacksonian Era

Even while states were moving toward denying free blacks the right to vote, the franchise was expanding for white men. All states admitted to the Union after 1815 adopted white male suffrage, and between 1807 and 1821, others abolished the property and tax qualifications for voting. These developments had a dramatic effect on national elections. Measuring voter turnout before the presidential election of 1824 is impossible because only electoral votes were counted, but in the 1824 presidential election, 355,000 popular votes were cast, and the number more than tripled—to more than 1.1 million—just four years later, in large part due to the end of property requirements.

The method of voting also began to change. Until the 1820s, a man voted by going to his precinct's voting place and orally stating his choices. The absence of a secret, written ballot allowed intimidation; few would vote against a particular candidate when the room was crowded with his supporters. Printed ballots gave the voter a more independent voice, even though the first ballots were published by the political parties themselves. A ballot printed by the government, the so-called **Australian ballot,** was not introduced until the late nineteenth century. Furthermore, many political offices became elective rather than appointive, making office holders more accountable to the public. By 1832, almost all the states (South Carolina was the sole exception) shifted the selection of members of the Electoral College from their legislature directly to the voters. In 1826, the provisions of the Maryland constitution that barred Jews from practicing law and holding public office were removed.

**The election of 1824.** The Era of Good Feelings came to an end with the presidential election of 1824. Although Republicans dominated national politics, the party was breaking apart internally. Monroe's cabinet included no fewer than three men with presidential ambitions, each representing sectional interests. John C. Calhoun and Secretary of the Treasury William Crawford contended for the role of spokesperson for the South, while Secretary of State John Quincy Adams promoted the interests of New England. Outside the cabinet, Speaker of the House Henry Clay stood for his "American System," and the military hero Andrew Jackson, the lone political outsider, championed western ideas.

Party leaders backed Crawford. Although a paralyzing stroke removed him from an active role in the campaign, he received almost as many votes as Clay. Calhoun removed himself from the race, settling for another term as vice president and making plans for another run at the presidency in 1828 or 1832. Jackson received 43 percent of the popular vote compared to Adams's 31 percent, and he won 99 electoral votes to Adams's 84. Because Jackson did not receive a majority in the Electoral College, the election was decided by the House of Representatives, where Speaker Clay exercised considerable political influence. With no chance of winning himself, Clay threw his support to Adams, who shared his nationalist views. Thirteen of the twenty-one states voted for Adams, and he became president. When Adams appointed Clay his secretary of state, Jackson's supporters angrily charged that a **"corrupt bargain"** had been made between the two men. Although there is no firm evidence to support the charge, it became an issue that hounded Adams during his presidency and was raised by Jackson himself during the next presidential campaign.

**The Adams presidency.** Few candidates were as qualified as John Quincy Adams to be president, yet few presidents have had such a disappointing term. In his first annual message to Congress (1825), he laid out an extensive program of federal spending that stretched even the most liberal definition of internal improvements. Among other things, Adams called for the creation of a national university and a national observatory. But the president faced determined opposition everywhere he turned, both from Jackson's backers and Calhoun, who filled Senate committees with men who did not support the administration's policies. When Adams asked Congress for funds to send a delegate to the Congress of Panama, a meeting of the newly independent nations of Latin America, southerners argued so vociferously against the idea that the conference had ended by the time money was actually appropriated. Adams did not help his own cause. Refusing to engage in partisan politics, he did not remove opponents from appointed office when he became president and thereby alienated his own supporters. His rather idealistic position earned him little backing for a second term.

Politics had an impact on one of the most important domestic issues—protective tariffs. The **Tariff of 1824** imposed duties on woolen goods, cotton, iron, and other finished products to protect textile mills in New England and industries in the mid-Atlantic states. Four years later, Congress raised tariffs to the highest level before the Civil War and increased taxes on imports of raw wool. The Jacksonians included the duties on raw material in the legislation to weaken Adams's support from the mid-Atlantic and northern states in the upcoming election. Indeed, Jacksonians believed the bill to be so onerous to different interest groups in different parts of the country that it had no chance of passing. But the **Tariff of 1828** did become law, and it was soon called the **Tariff of Abominations**.

**The election of 1828.** The factionalism within the Republican ranks led to a split and the creation of two parties—Jackson's Democratic Republicans (soon shortened to "Democrats") and Adams's National Republicans. Martin Van Buren of New York, who preferred rivalries between parties to disputes within one party, masterminded the emergence of the Democrats.

The campaign itself was less about issues than the character of the two candidates. Jacksonians denounced Adams for being "an aristocrat" and for allegedly trying to influence Russian policy by providing Tsar Alexander I with an American prostitute during Adams's term as ambassador. Supporters of Adams vilified Jackson as a murderer (he had fought several duels), an adulterer (he and his wife had mistakenly married before her divorce from her first husband was final), and an illiterate backwoodsman. These attacks by the National Republicans did little to detract from Jackson's popularity. Ordinary Americans admired his leadership qualities and decisiveness; they preferred to remember Jackson the Indian fighter and hero of the Battle of New Orleans and forget about the important role Adams played in negotiating the Treaty of Ghent, which ended the War of 1812. Jackson also had clear political advantages. As a westerner, he had secure support from that part of the country, while the fact that he was a slave owner gave him strength in the South. Conversely, Adams was strong only in New England. Jackson was swept into office with 56 percent of the popular vote from a greatly expanded electorate.

## Jackson as President

Jackson's inauguration celebration proved unlike that of any previous president. Long before 1829, Washington, D.C., had developed a code of proper behavior for such occasions, and the rowdy crowd that mobbed the White House to cheer on the new president left the city's social arbiters aghast. Many of those attending the inauguration were looking for jobs. Jackson mentioned **"rotation in office"**—the dismissal of rival-party officeholders and installment of political supporters in their places—in his inaugural address. Although he did not invent the practice, he endorsed the rotation that his critics called the **"spoils system,"** and his administration became identified with it. But Jackson did not make wholesale replacements when he became president, and the turnover during his two terms was rather modest. In any event, he relied more heavily on political allies, newspaper editors, and friends for advice. The only member of his informal advisory group, called the **Kitchen Cabinet,** who came from within government was Secretary of State Martin Van Buren.

With presidential aspirations of his own, Van Buren used his influence to weaken Vice President John Calhoun over the issue of internal improvements. It was Van Buren who drafted Jackson's veto message on the **Maysville Road bill,** which would have provided indirect federal funding for a road entirely within the state of Kentucky. Politics aside, the veto probably had less to do with Jackson's opposition to internal improvements and more with the fact that the legislation primarily benefited a single state. Indeed, during Jackson's presidency, more money was spent annually on developing the nation's infrastructure than under Adams.

**The Eaton affair.** The rift between Jackson and Calhoun went beyond new roads; it was personal. When John H. Eaton, Jackson's secretary of war, married a widowed waitress named Peggy O'Neale, the wives of the other cabinet members refused to receive her socially. Jackson was particularly sensitive to such snubs; he blamed the death of his own wife, Rachel, shortly after he took office on the vicious attacks against her during the 1828 campaign. He confronted Floride Calhoun as the leader of Washington's social set, and their arguments became so bitter that they contributed to the estrangement between Jackson and his vice president. The situation flared into open hostility during the nullification controversy.

**The nullification controversy.** To southerners, who depended more on imports than any other region of the country, the Tariff of 1828 was both discriminatory and unconstitutional. Calhoun responded to it by drafting the *South Carolina Exposition and Protest,* which introduced the idea that states had the right to **nullify** (refuse to obey) any law passed by Congress they considered unjust. Jackson supported protective tariffs but agreed to a slight reduction in rates in 1832. The change did not go far enough for Calhoun. He resigned the vice presidency in protest and returned to South Carolina, whose legislature promptly sent him back to Washington as a senator.

Calhoun claimed that the only tariff permitted by the Constitution was one that raised money for the common good. Tariffs that adversely affected the economy of one part of the nation (the South) while benefiting other regions (New England and the mid-Atlantic states) were unconstitutional. In November 1832, South Carolina passed an ordinance of nullification that forbade customs duties from being collected in its port cities under the new tariff.

Jackson wasted no time in moving against South Carolina. He proclaimed nullification itself unconstitutional, stressed that the Constitution had created a single nation rather than a group of states, and threatened to use force to collect the customs duties. The forts in Charleston harbor were put on alert by the secretary of war, and federal troops in South Carolina were prepared for action. Military confrontation was prevented through the efforts of Henry Clay, who for the second time in his career achieved a major political compromise. Congress passed two bills in March 1833, both approved by Jackson, that ultimately defused the situation. The **Compromise Tariff** gradually reduced duties over a ten-year period, and the **Force Bill** authorized the president to enforce federal law in South Carolina by military means, if necessary. South Carolina withdrew its tariff nullification ordinance, crediting Clay's leadership rather than Jackson's threats. The solution was general enough that both Jackson and Calhoun claimed the victory.

**The bank crisis.** Jackson hated banks, paper money, and anyone who profited from them. Most of his ire was directed at the Second Bank of the United States because it was controlled by private interests and acted as a creditor of state banks. As the depository of federal revenues, it was able to lend money far beyond the capability of state institutions and require them to repay their loans in hard currency, not their own notes.

Established in 1816, the Second Bank was due for a new charter in 1836. Nicholas Biddle, its president, tried to get the bank rechartered four years ahead of the expiration. He was backed by Clay, who hoped to use the bank as an issue in his bid for the presidency in 1832. Congress passed the necessary legislation by a significant margin, but Jackson vetoed the bill, and its supporters did not have enough votes to override. Denouncing the early rechartering scheme, Jackson condemned the bank as a privileged monopoly that gave a few men far too much power. Even though the bank had been upheld by the Supreme Court (in *McCulloch* v. *Maryland,* 1819) and clearly had strong support in Congress, Jackson still considered the bank unconstitutional. His overwhelming electoral victory in 1832 gave him the political clout to take further action.

Not long into his second term, Jackson ordered that the operating expenses of the federal government be paid out of the existing deposits in the Second Bank and that new federal revenues be placed in selected state banks. These state banks became known as **"pet" banks.** The short-term results of this policy were twofold. Even though the Second Bank's charter would expire in 1836 by its own terms, withdrawing from the funds already in the bank and discontinuing federal deposits bled the bank dry. Meanwhile, shifting federal deposits to the state banks empowered them to print more notes and make more loans.

Jackson's criterion for state banks to become pet banks was loyalty to the Democratic party, but his original intention to limit their number was thwarted by the banks' pressing for federal deposits. By the end of 1833, there were twenty-three pet banks. The banks issued paper money backed by federal gold and lent it to speculators to buy federal lands. Public land sales grew rapidly, and to stop excessive speculation, Jackson issued the **"Specie Circular"** in 1836. It required that public land be purchased with gold or silver, not paper notes. While speculation was reduced, the new policy drew criticism from westerners, for whom hard currency was scarce. In the long run, Jackson's actions on the banks contributed to a serious economic crisis, which the president left for his hand-picked successor to shoulder.

## Martin Van Buren and New Political Alignments

By 1834, a new political coalition had emerged in opposition to Jackson's policies. Led by Daniel Webster of Massachusetts and Henry Clay of Virginia, the members called themselves the **Whigs.** Just as the Whigs during the American Revolution stood up to the tyranny of King George III, the new Whigs challenged what they considered to be the abuse of presidential power by "King Andrew I." They drew their support from New England, the mid-Atlantic states, and the upper Midwest and from southern planters who broke with the Democrats over nullification and those who favored internal improvements and high tariffs. The Whig economic program was attractive to the country's industrial and commercial elite and successful farmers. Reform advocates who called for an expansion of public education and those who wanted social change also found a political home among the Whigs. The Democrats' base was in the South and the West, particularly among the middle class and the small farmers. Those who felt their opportunity to advance was limited by the forces of monopoly and privilege—groups aligned with Jackson's attack on the Second Bank of the United States—also backed the Democrats, as did recent immigrants. Although Jackson clearly strengthened the office of the president, it was the Whigs who favored an activist national government, while the Democrats wanted greater state and local autonomy.

The **Anti-Masonic party** also joined ranks with the Whigs. It was the first third party in American politics and was established around a single issue—the claim that the Freemasons, a secret fraternal society that had counted George Washington among its members, were behind an anti-Christian, antidemocratic conspiracy to take over the government at all levels. The party's candidate in 1832 was chosen through the first nominating convention, and he won seven electoral votes.

**The election of 1836.** Despite what the Whigs may have thought of Jackson's "royal" ambitions, he honored the two-term tradition and bestowed his blessing on Vice President Martin Van Buren as the Democratic candidate in 1836. The Whigs, unable to decide on a single candidate, ran four men under their banner: William Henry Harrison, Hugh L. White, Daniel Webster, and W. P. Magnum. The idea was to prevent Van Buren from capturing a majority of the electoral vote and to throw the election into the House of Representatives, as in 1824. While the popular vote was very close (51 percent to 49 percent in favor of the Democrats, which was a sign of the growing Whig strength), Van Buren received 170 electoral votes to the combined Whig total of 124. None of the vice-presidential candidates, however, had a majority of the vote, and for the first and only time, that choice was left up to the Senate.

**The Panic of 1837.** No sooner had Van Buren taken office than an economic crisis gripped the nation. Although known as the Panic of 1837, economic conditions in the country remained unsettled for his entire term as president. The pet banks had been too generous in issuing paper notes and making loans; when the economy contracted and prices fell (cotton prices dropped by half in March 1837), the banks found that they could not make payouts in the hard currency that was supposed to have backed their notes, while their borrowers were defaulting on their loans. The sale of public lands declined sharply, and unemployment and prices for food and fuel rose. Estimates are that a third of Americans were out of work by late 1837, and many more were able to find only part-time jobs.

Van Buren tried to address the economic problems by using the Independent Treasury to hold government deposits and revenues. The **Independent Treasury** was not really a bank but simply a depository for federal gold and silver. Its creation and use meant that the money it stored was not available to banks to make loans; it also meant that hard currency that might have been used to stimulate the economy was kept out of circulation.

**The election of 1840.** Even though Van Buren was blamed for the depression (he was nicknamed "Van Ruin"), the Democrats nominated him for a second term. The Whigs united behind William Henry Harrison and balanced the ticket with John Tyler of Virginia, a Democrat who had broken with Jackson over nullification. While the Whigs did not present a formal platform, the Democrats put a plank in theirs opposing congressional interference with slavery. This was the first time a political party took a position on the "peculiar institution," and it was done both in response to a growing abolitionist sentiment in the North and simply to reflect the position of the Democratic constituency in the South. But the campaign itself was not about issues.

The election of 1840 earned the name the "Campaign of Tomfoolery." Voters cast their ballots more for personality than anything else. When Democrats made the mistake of saying that all Harrison wanted to do was sit in a log cabin and sip cider, the Whigs made the most of it. Their rallies featured portable log cabins with roofs that opened to reveal jugs of hard cider for thirsty voters. Indeed, the Whigs did everything they could to portray Harrison as a latter-day Jackson. He was a frontiersman (even though he had attended a university and studied medicine) and military hero. The campaign slogan "Tippecanoe and Tyler Too!" was intended to remind voters of Harrison's victory against the tribes in the Old Northwest. Conversely, Van Buren, who was the closest thing to a professional politician the country had yet produced, was effectively painted as an aristocrat who dined off fine china in the palatial White House.

The serious economic problems and the "log cabin and cider campaign" had their effect. More than 80 percent of the nation's eligible voters participated in the election of 1840. Harrison defeated Van Buren 234 electoral votes to 60 and took 53 percent of the popular vote. Van Buren was unable to carry even his home state of New York. With his defeat, the era of Jacksonian politics came to an end. For twenty years (1836–56), the Whigs and the Democrats, both of which were truly national parties, were fairly evenly matched in the political arena, although the growing split between North and South over slavery after 1840 weakened party loyalties and changed the party system.

## Assessing Jacksonian Democracy

During the period from 1824 to 1840, the American political system came of age. Not only were more men eligible to vote, but an increasing percentage of the eligible were actually exercising their right to do so. Political parties, which the framers of the Constitution made no provision for and disdained, became an established fact of American life. Elements of the process by which presidents are chosen—the party convention and the party platform—were introduced. Even if the parties did not focus on the major questions of the day (most notably slavery), the campaigns they ran were geared to bring out as many people as possible to support a candidate.

Jackson probably viewed his two terms as president a success. He had resolved the problem of the Native American tribes east of the Mississippi River. The removal was nearing completion by the time he left office. He had forcefully met the challenge posed by nullification and, perhaps most important to him, had brought an end to the Second Bank of the United States. But the long-term influence of Jackson was less in his specific policies and more in the way he carried them out. The Whig characterization of Jackson as "King Andrew I" contrasted sharply with the idea that he represented the common man, but more important, it demonstrated that the presidency had changed under him. In the nullification controversy, he made full use of the power granted him under the Constitution and discovered that the veto and the knowledge that a president would use it was an effective tool in shaping policy. Just as the Whigs and Democrats pioneered the techniques of modern two-party politics, Jackson pointed the way toward the modern presidency.

The political system did not address the matter of equality outside the group of white males who were citizens of the United States. But movements calling for the abolition of slavery and for women's rights emerged before the middle of the century, while other reform programs addressed the social ills that came with an increasingly urban and industrial society.

The term **antebellum,** "before the war," is often used by historians to refer to the decades before the Civil War in the United States. "Antebellum" creates an image of a time when slavery was not only legal but an integral part of life in the South, when the first spurt of industrialization occurred in the United States, and when Americans explored and settled the trans-Mississippi West. The antebellum decades were also a period during which another religious revival swept the country, reformers sought to address many of the social questions that the politicians would not or could not, and American culture, defined through its literature and art, came into its own.

## The Religious Revival

Beginning in the 1790s and continuing into the 1840s, evangelical Christianity once again became an important factor in American life. Revivalism began in earnest at the edge of the frontier with **circuit riders,** or itinerant preachers, bringing their message to isolated farms and small settlements. Open-air camp meetings, which could last as long as four days and attract more than ten thousand people from the surrounding countryside, were often characterized by emotional outbursts—wild gestures and speaking in tongues—from the participants. The number of women who converted at these meetings was much larger than the number of men, an indication of women's increasing role as defenders of the spiritual values in the home. The Methodist denomination, which was the driving force behind this so-called Second Great Awakening (the Great Awakening is discussed on pages 36–37), grew from seventy thousand members in 1800 to more than one million in 1844, making it the largest Protestant group in the country.

**The "Burned-Over District."** After its first sweep along the frontier, revivalism moved back east. So many fiery revivals were held in western New York during the 1820s that the region became known as the **"Burned-Over District."** Foremost among the New York preachers was Charles G. Finney, who found a receptive audience in the rapidly growing and changing communities along the Erie Canal. Finney rejected such formal doctrines as predestination and original sin and emphasized that every person is free to choose between good and evil. Conversion to him was not just an individual decision to avoid drunkenness, fornication, and other sins; if enough people found salvation, Finney believed, society as a whole would be reformed.

Despite its gains for the church rolls, the Second Great Awakening was not without its critics. The Unitarians, who included the well-educated and wealthy elite of New England among their members, declared the revivals far too emotional and questioned the sincerity of the conversion experience. While the Methodists emphasized the "heart" over the "head," Unitarianism stressed reason, free will, and individual moral responsibility.

**The Mormons.** A new religious group also came out of the Burned-Over District: the Church of Jesus Christ of Latter-day Saints, whose supporters were called **Mormons.** Its founder was Joseph Smith, who claimed that he was led by the angel Moroni to decipher the Book of Mormon, which told of the migration of ancient Hebrews to America and the founding of the true church. Smith and his followers faced persecution wherever they went because of their radical teachings, particularly their endorsement of polygamy. The Mormons settled in Nauvoo, Illinois, in 1839, but Smith and his brother were killed by an angry mob in 1844. Leadership of the church passed to Brigham Young.

In 1847, Young led about fifteen thousand Mormons to the valley of Great Salt Lake and began to develop what he called the state of Deseret, which was organized as the Utah Territory by Congress in 1850. Young became the territorial governor, and although he was removed from the position during his second term because of an ongoing dispute between the Mormons and the federal government over polygamy, he remained the political as well as religious leader of the Mormons until his death.

**The Shaker community.** Founded in England in the 1770s by Mother Ann Lee, the Shakers opposed materialism and believed in an imminent Second Coming. They found converts in the Burned-Over District and, during their heyday from the 1820s to the 1840s, established communities from Massachusetts to Ohio. The Shakers did not believe in marriage or the family, and the ultimate decline of the group was due to their practicing celibacy. The Shakers are remembered for their spiritual values and their craftsmanship, particularly in their simple furniture designs, but their otherworldliness set them apart from the Protestant sects that accepted material success as compatible with religion.

## The Impulse for Reform

In the first half of the nineteenth century, politicians either ignored or avoided a number of social issues, including alcoholism, the quality of public education, slavery, and women's rights. Reformers, working as individuals and through organizations, were left to tackle these problems.

**The temperance movement.** By the early nineteenth century, the per capita consumption of hard liquor (whiskey, brandy, rum, and gin) had grown dramatically to more than five gallons a year. The high level of consumption was blamed for poverty: workingmen spent their wages on alcohol instead of rent or food and were frequently absent from their factory jobs. Alcohol abuse also contributed to the abuse of wives and children. In 1826, the American Temperance Society began a persistent campaign against the evils of drinking. Although focusing at first on persuading individuals to abstain, the advocates of temperance soon entered the political arena and sought laws to limit the sale and manufacture of alcohol. The movement caught on—particularly in New England but much less so in the South—and by the 1840s, national consumption had dropped to half of what it had been two decades earlier. The reformers were not satisfied, however, and they continued to press for a complete ban on the sale and use of all intoxicating liquor, an effort that culminated in the 1919 passage of the Eighteenth Amendment, ushering in the era of Prohibition.

**Improving public education.** The demand for free public education grew during the 1830s as the franchise expanded. Education was deemed important for creating an informed electorate. In addition, factory workers wanted their children to have more opportunities than they had had, and schooling was seen as a way to assimilate the children of immigrants through the inculcation of American values.

Already-existing schools generally taught the "three Rs"—reading, writing, and arithmetic—to a room full of boys and girls whose ages might have run from three to eighteen. Reformers found that system inadequate for preparing students to succeed in a rapidly changing society. Massachusetts, as it had during the early colonial period, took the lead in promoting education. In 1827, the state passed a law that provided for the establishment of high schools and set guidelines for curricula based on community size. The legislation was strictly enforced after Horace Mann was appointed the first secretary of the Massachusetts State Board of Education in 1837. During his tenure, state funding for schools increased, new high schools were established, compulsory school attendance laws were passed, a specified school term (six months) was delineated, and structured curricula and teacher training were designed and implemented. Mann also called for "grade" schools that would use a placement system based on the age and skills of the students.

Massachusetts pioneered popular education in addition to public education. The state was the birthplace of the **lyceum** (1826), an organization that attracted large audiences for its public lectures on literature, art, and science. Many of the lyceums that were developed across the country during the 1830s and 1840s also had lending libraries with books for children as well as adults.

One of the results of the changes to education was an increase in women teachers. The first high school for girls was opened in New York in 1821, and Oberlin College was established as a coeducational institution in 1833. Mount Holyoke was founded as a women's college four years later. Educational reform was more successful in the North than in the South, where even white illiteracy was high. African Americans did not benefit from improvements in public education. Free blacks attended poor segregated schools, and slaves generally received no formal education at all. Notably, one institution of higher learning, again Oberlin College, admitted blacks as well as women.

**The abolitionist movement.** Congress considered slavery so controversial that in 1836, the House of Representatives, largely at the insistence of southerners, passed a gag rule prohibiting discussion or debate of the subject. This move was a reaction to numerous petitions submitted to Congress that called for the abolition of slavery and the slave trade in the District of Columbia, a reflection of a growing antislavery movement in the United States.

Not all Americans who opposed slavery favored simply putting an end to it. Some considered slavery to be wrong but were unwilling to take action against it, while others accepted slavery in the states where it already existed but opposed its expansion into new territories. An early antislavery proposal was to repatriate slaves to Africa. Farfetched as it seems, in 1822, under the auspices of the American Colonization Society, the first freed slaves departed for what would become the independent nation of Liberia in West Africa. Over the next forty years, however, only about fifteen thousand blacks emigrated to Liberia, a number far below the natural increase in the slave population that accounted for most of the population's growth before the Civil War.

Advocates of an immediate end to slavery were known as **abolitionists.** The movement's chief spokesperson was William Lloyd

Garrison, who began publishing his antislavery newspaper, the *Liberator,* in 1831. His American Anti-Slavery Society (organized in 1833) called for the "immediate abandonment" of slavery without compensation to slaveholders; the end to the domestic slave trade; and, radically, the recognition of the equality of blacks and whites. The abolitionists, however, were divided on how best to achieve these goals. While Garrison opposed political action, moderate abolitionists formed the Liberty party and ran James G. Birney for president in 1840. The party's strength was such that it determined the outcome of the presidential election four years later. The movement split, however, in 1840 over the appropriate role of women within the organization. Even though women, such as Angelina and Sarah Grimké, were deeply committed to the cause, many members of the society felt it was inappropriate for women to speak before predominantly male audiences. More important, there was significant opposition to the inclusion of women's rights issues under the umbrella of the abolitionist program.

Free blacks were the strongest supporters of the abolitionist movement and its most effective speakers. Escaped slaves like Frederick Douglass provided northerners with vivid firsthand accounts of slavery, and his book *Narrative of the Life of Frederick Douglass* (1845) was just one of many slave autobiographies popular in abolitionist circles. While most blacks supported a peaceful end to slavery, some believed that only insurrection could actually bring it about.

**Beginnings of the women's rights movement.** The various reform movements of the nineteenth century gave women—particularly, middle-class women—an opportunity to participate in public life, and they were mainly successful in their efforts. A prime example is the work by Dorothea Dix to create public mental-health institutions that would provide humane care for the insane. American women turned their attention to their own situation when activists split from the abolitionists. The specific event that led to the organized push for women's rights was the exclusion of a group of American women from the 1840 World Anti-Slavery Convention in London. One hundred women met in Seneca Falls, New York, in 1848, led by Elizabeth Cady Stanton and Lucretia Mott, both abolitionist activists, to draft a statement of women's rights. The Seneca Falls **"Declaration of Sentiments and Resolutions"** called for equality for women before the law, including changes in divorce laws that automatically gave custody of children to the husband. Equal employment opportunity and the right to vote were other important demands.

The only women's rights issue that was addressed before the Civil War concerned property. Several states, but far from all, gave married women control over inherited property during the antebellum period. Women did not get the right to vote until 1920 (through the Nineteenth Amendment), and they were still limited to careers in either teaching or nursing. It took more than a century for the issues of equal employment and full legal and social equality to be seriously addressed.

**The utopian communities.** During the period from about 1820 to 1850, a number of people thought that creating utopian communities, which would serve as models for the world, could solve society's ills better than the reform movements. All of these utopian communities failed, usually because of the imperfections in those seeking perfection. For example, British industrialist Robert Owen, who knew firsthand the evils of the factory system, established **New Harmony** (Indiana) in 1825 as a planned community based on a balance of agriculture and manufacturing. The nine hundred men and women who went there either refused to work or quarreled among themselves, and New Harmony collapsed after just a few years. French Socialist Charles Fourier's idea for small mixed-economy cooperatives known as **phalanxes** also caught on in the United States. **Brook Farm** (1841–46) in Massachusetts, perhaps the best-known utopian experiment because it attracted support from writers Ralph Waldo Emerson and Nathaniel Hawthorne, combined manual labor with intellectual pursuits and became a phalanx in 1844.

Utopian communities were also founded by religious groups. John Humphrey Noyes, a product of the Second Great Awakening, and disciples of the Society of Inquiry founded the **Oneida Community** in New York in 1848. In contrast to the celibate Shakers, Noyes's followers accepted "complex marriage," the idea that every man and every woman in the community were married to each other. Boys and girls were trained in sexual practices when they reached puberty, but only those who accepted Jesus Christ as their savior were allowed to have sexual relations. Oneida prospered because it developed products known for their quality, first steel traps and later silver flatware. When Noyes left Oneida to avoid prosecution for adultery, the members abandoned complex marriage and formed a company to continue manufacturing tableware. It remains in business today as Oneida Community, Ltd.

## Literature and Art in Antebellum America

In the first half of the nineteenth century, an American national literature was born. Naturally accompanying it was the first American reference work, Noah Webster's *American Dictionary of the English Language,* published in 1828. While Webster's work did not create American English, the dictionary did declare the independence of American usage. Webster insisted on using American spellings, such as "plow" for "plough"; taking the "u" out of such words as "labour" and "honour"; and writing definitions taken from American life.

Another important literary milestone was Ralph Waldo Emerson's "American Scholar," an address he gave at Harvard in 1837. At a time when many in the United States remained in awe of European culture, he argued that Americans were self-reliant enough to develop a literature reflecting their own national character. "Our day of dependence, our long apprenticeship to the learning of other lands, draws to a close," he told his audience. Emerson espoused **transcendentalism,** which proclaimed that intuition and experience provided knowledge and truth just as effectively as did the intellect, that man is innately good, and that there is unity in the entire creation.

Emerson's "American Scholar" speech and transcendentalism both influenced and reflected an impressive flowering of American literature. The country's literary centers were New England and New York. From New England came the historical works of George Bancroft (*History of the United States*, ten volumes, the first published in 1834), Francis Parkman (*The Oregon Trail*, 1849), and William H. Prescott (*History of the Conquest of Mexico*, 1843) as well as the poetry of Henry Wadsworth Longfellow, John Greenleaf Whittier, and Emily Dickinson (although Dickinson did most of her writing after the Civil War). Emerson, Nathaniel Hawthorne, Henry David Thoreau, and Margaret Fuller were the region's most noted authors. New York produced Washington Irving, James Fenimore Cooper, Herman Melville, and Walt Whitman; Edgar Allen Poe, though born in Virginia, did most of his writing in New York and Philadelphia.

**James Fenimore Cooper.** Cooper was among the first writers to appreciate the value of the frontier as a distinctly American literary setting. Beginning with the *Pioneers* (1823), he created a body of work that celebrates the courage and adventuresomeness of the American character and explores the conflict between the wilderness and the advance of civilization. His five novels featuring the frontiersman Natty Bumppo, collectively known as the "Leatherstocking Tales" and including such classics as the *Last of the Mohicans* (1826) and the *Deerslayer* (1841), were all bestsellers. Cooper portrayed nature as something to be used but protected and not conquered.

**Henry David Thoreau.** Thoreau's fame rests on two works, neither of which received much attention during his lifetime. *Walden* (1854) is an account of two years he spent in his cabin near Walden Pond in Massachusetts. The stay was an experiment in self-sufficiency, a reaction to what the transcendentalists saw as growing commercialism and materialism in American society. Although Thoreau did not completely cut himself off from civilization during his stay, he believed that only in nature could individuals really understand themselves and the purpose of life.

In 1846, Thoreau refused to pay his poll tax as a protest against the Mexican War, which he, like many abolitionists, saw as nothing more than an attempt to expand slavery. He spent one night in jail before the tax was paid by a relative. To explain his actions, he wrote "Civil Disobedience" (1849), stating, "The only obligation which I have a right to assume, is to do at any time what I think right," a position that reflected the individualism of the transcendentalists taken to an extreme. Although ignored in the nineteenth century, Thoreau's discourse influenced Mahatma Gandhi in his struggle for the independence of India and the American civil rights leaders of the 1950s and 1960s.

**Walt Whitman.** In 1855, Whitman published the first edition of *Leaves of Grass*, which he continued to revise, rearrange, and enlarge until his death in 1892. A revolutionary work that greatly influenced American poetry, it expressed Whitman's love for his country in lusty and controversial free verse that included homoerotic images. While many critics at the time found *Leaves* crude and vulgar, Emerson found Whitman's poetry to be decidedly American, democratic and plain. Whitman shared Thoreau's abolitionist sentiments, but the two parted company on politics; Whitman had an unbridled faith in democratic government, despite its imperfections.

**Hawthorne, Melville, and Poe.** Nathaniel Hawthorne was fascinated by the dark side of the Puritan mind. His novels, especially the *Scarlet Letter* (1850) and the *House of Seven Gables* (1851), dealt with revenge, guilt, and pride. Although he had been involved with Brook Farm and wrote the *Blithedale Romance* (1852) based on his experiences there, Hawthorne did not share the transcendentalists' faith in the perfectibility of man.

Herman Melville, unlike many of the writers before the Civil War, did not receive recognition for his work while he was alive. His first novels, *Typee* (1846) and *Omoo* (1847), were set in the South Pacific, where he had visited as a sailor. *Moby-Dick* (1851), based on

Melville's experiences on a whaling ship, was not appreciated as one of the great works of American fiction until the 1920s.

Edgar Allan Poe focused on literary genres different from those of his contemporaries: the short story and short poem. His work reflected his own pessimistic outlook on life and focused chiefly on the mental state of the characters. He is credited with pioneering detective fiction in such stories as the "Murders in the Rue Morgue" (1843) and gothic horror in the "Fall of the House of Usher" (1839) and the "Tell-Tale Heart" (1843).

**American art.** In the decades before the Civil War, a distinctive style of American landscape painting attracted considerable attention. The **Hudson River school,** comprising such artists as Thomas Cole, Frederic Church, and Asher Durand, captured on canvas the massive trees, sparkling water, and lush American environment, conveying a sense of the majesty and mystery of the wilderness that was quickly disappearing. Just as Emerson had claimed that Americans should write about themselves in their own place, Cole noted in an essay published in 1836 that it was not necessary for artists to go to Europe to find subjects for their paintings: "American scenery... has features, and glorious ones, unknown to Europe. The most distinctive, and perhaps the most impressive, characteristic of American scenery is its wildness."

## Recreation and Leisure in Antebellum America

During the antebellum period, popular pastimes included a variety of participant and spectator sports. The *New York Clipper,* a magazine first published in 1853, employed a network of reporters spread across the country who used the new electric telegraph to cover every kind of sport, including foot races, pedestrian (walking) events, horse races, dog fights, cock fights, rat catching, boxing matches, rowing regattas, and, of course, baseball games.

Although the myth persists that Abner Doubleday invented baseball in 1839 in Cooperstown, New York, the game actually evolved from the English sport called "rounders" and was played in the colonies during the eighteenth century. Credit for key changes to what was variously called "town ball," "four-old cat," and "base ball" belongs to Alexander Cartwright. In 1845, he suggested that runners be tagged with the ball rather than hit with it and that each team be limited to three outs. These rules led to modern baseball, which was on its way to becoming a national pastime by the Civil War.

**Popular reading.** Improvements made to printing presses had a dramatic impact on Americans' reading. As technology reduced production costs, allowing publishers to sell newspapers for a penny an issue, readership increased. The number of newspapers in the country grew from fewer than one hundred in 1790 to more than thirty-seven hundred by 1860. Large metropolitan papers, such as the *New York Sun* and the *New York Herald,* featured sensational stories about crime, sex, and scandal. The number of magazines also began to grow in the second half of the nineteenth century. "Highbrow" periodicals, such as the *North American Review* and *Harper's,* which is still in print today, carried articles by some of the most noted authors of the day, while other magazines catered to the tastes and interests of specific audiences—women, farmers, and businessmen, for example.

The expansion of public education, the opening of lending libraries, and the popularity of the lyceum created a mass audience for books. Although the works of Cooper and Hawthorne sold well, even more popular were sentimental novels by and for women, books that provided advice or practical instruction (early "how-to" books), and literature with a moral message. Often, books were serialized in newspapers or magazines before they were published as full novels. Such was the case with Harriet Beecher Stowe's bestseller *Uncle Tom's Cabin* (1852), which was written in response to the Fugitive Slave Law of 1850 and did much to strengthen antislavery sentiment in the North.

**Theater and P. T. Barnum.** The theater was as popular in antebellum America as movies are today. Best-selling novels were adapted for the stage; *Uncle Tom's Cabin* was produced in New York in 1853, for example (interestingly, African Americans had to enter the theater through a special entrance and were segregated from the rest of the audience). Shakespeare's plays were a perennial favorite, as were melodramas and comedies. Shows that touched on the social issues of the day were important. Temperance plays, which showed how alcohol could destroy a family, were a popular genre, and about fifty plays about Native Americans were staged between 1825 and 1860.

Early in his career as a showman, Phineas T. Barnum realized that people would pay to see exotic and sensational exhibits purported to have an educational value. In 1835, he introduced the public to an aged black woman, Joice Heth, who he claimed had been George Washington's nurse. Barnum followed this hoax with the "Feejee mermaid," created by sewing together a fish and the upper body of a monkey. The "mermaid" and other odd displays, along with appearances by the famous twenty-five-inch-tall dwarf, General Tom Thumb, were featured attractions at Barnum's American Museum in New York City (1842). Barnum was also a legitimate theatrical promoter; he brought the noted Swedish singer Jenny Lind to the United States for a concert tour in 1850.

**The impact of the minstrel shows.** One of the most popular forms of entertainment beginning in the 1840s was the **minstrel show,** which featured white performers acting out skits, singing, dancing, and telling jokes in blackface makeup. African Americans were consistently portrayed either as clumsy, lazy, stupid, docile, and childlike or as arrogant and dandified, looking ridiculous as they tried to adopt white ways. The extreme stereotypes that the shows and their advertising conveyed reflected the strong racial prejudice in the United States. Minstrel shows confirmed whites' sense of superiority while providing a racial justification for slavery. Curiously, the shows were popular at a time when feelings against slavery in the North had been increasing.

Long after the heyday of minstrel shows passed, American audiences could still see vaudeville entertainers such as Eddie Cantor and Al Jolson in blackface, and the tradition continued into the era of sound motion pictures. Even African-American stage actors often had to undergo the indignity of putting on the distinctive makeup because theatrical convention required it.

At the time of the American revolution, slavery was a national institution; although the number of slaves was small, they lived and worked in every colony. Even before the Constitution was ratified, however, states in the North were either abolishing slavery outright or passing laws providing for gradual emancipation. The Northwest Ordinance of 1787 barred slavery from the new territories of that period, so rather quickly, slavery effectively existed only in the South and became that region's "peculiar institution."

## Slavery, the Economy, and Society in the South

Between the first federal census in 1790 and the eve of the Civil War, the slave population in the United States increased from approximately seven hundred thousand to almost four million. The formal end to the foreign slave trade in 1808 had no impact—the smuggling of slaves was common—and in any event, natural increase accounted for practically all of the slave-population growth in the United States. The nationwide distribution of slaves also changed during this time span. Around 1820, slavery was concentrated in the tobacco-growing areas of Virginia, North Carolina, and Kentucky and along the coasts of South Carolina and northern Georgia. By 1860, it had significantly expanded into the Deep South, particularly Georgia, Alabama, Mississippi, Louisiana, and Texas, following the spread of cotton production. Had slavery somehow ceased during that expansion, it would have been impossible for the South to meet the worldwide demand for its products.

**The Cotton Kingdom.** Cotton production was originally limited because separating the seeds from the fiber of the particular plant variety that grew well across most of the South was a time-consuming process. The introduction of the cotton gin resolved this problem and made the use of large numbers of field hands to work the crop economical. The invention came along just as the soil in the older tobacco-growing regions of the South was nearly depleted but about the time the removal of Native Americans from the very lands where cotton grew best had begun.

The principal source of slaves for the Cotton Kingdom was the Upper South, which included the states traditionally considered to be border states—Delaware, Maryland, and Kentucky—as well as Missouri, Virginia, North Carolina, Tennessee, and Arkansas. Agriculture in this part of the South was diversifying, and although tobacco and rice remained staple cash crops, more and more acreage was being devoted to wheat, corn, rye, and oats for local consumption. Half of the country's corn was grown in the South. These cereal grains were not as labor intensive as cotton or tobacco, and planters in the region were finding themselves with more slaves than they needed. Alexandria, Virginia, became a major center of the internal slave trade, and according to one estimate, three hundred thousand slaves were sold from there into the Deep South in the two decades before the Civil War.

**Slavery as an economic institution.** A small percentage of slaves were domestic servants, working in a planter's main house as cooks, nursemaids, seamstresses, and coachmen. An even smaller percentage worked as laborers or craftsmen—carpenters, masons, and blacksmiths. It was not unheard of for "spare" slaves to become mill or factory workers, and skilled artisans might be hired out to other plantations by their masters. But the overwhelming majority of slaves were field hands, picking cotton and planting and harvesting rice, tobacco, and sugar cane. The occupational distribution of slaves reflected the nature of the economy and society of the South, a region that was agricultural and rural with very little industrialization and urbanization compared to the North.

Irrespective of the jobs that slaves did, slavery on the whole was profitable. The expense to planters for housing, clothing, and feeding slaves was considerably less than the value they produced. Estimates vary, but expenses associated with the maintenance of one field hand were probably half the value of the revenue the master received from the slave's labor. Profitability increased steadily in the first half of the nineteenth century, as prices for cash crops rose and the cost of keeping slaves remained level. The slaves themselves became a good investment. As cotton production expanded and the demand for slaves increased, their prices rose accordingly. The highest prices were paid for "prime field hands," usually healthy young men in their late teens and twenties, but women with like agricultural skills were often sold for the same amounts. The enterprising slave owner bought and sold slaves for an additional source of income.

**Planters.** The image of the South as a place where plantation adjoined plantation and the entire white population owned slaves is a myth. Three quarters of the southern whites owned no slaves at all, and among those that did, most owned fewer than ten. Although the **planter class,** those individuals who owned twenty or more slaves to work plantations of about a thousand acres, was extremely small, it comprised the southern elite. (A very few plantations were several thousand acres in size and used hundreds of slaves.) With the day-to-day routine of the plantation in the hands of an overseer, a planter had little contact with his slaves except for those working in his house. The planter was an agrarian businessman, deciding how much land to put into cash crops versus foodstuffs, debating whether to buy more slaves or invest in machinery, and always keeping an eye on the market prices of his crops. Wealth, social position, and lifestyle separated the planter from the farmer who owned just a few slaves and usually labored alongside them in the fields. However, the goal of many small slaveholding farmers was to obtain more slaves and land so they could become planters themselves.

The "cult of domesticity" took root in the South as well as the North but with regional differences. A southern planter's wife had many more people to look after in her household than her immediate family. She supervised the work of the domestic slaves, looked after the upkeep of the slave quarters, served as nurse and seamstress (ready-made clothes were less available in the South than in the North), and maintained the household accounts. While southern women were expected to be models of virtue, the men were bound by no such standards. Southern women endured the disappointment and humiliation of seeing mulatto children on the plantation who had been fathered by their husbands and sons. No laws protected slaves from rape by their owners, nor did the white men face any social consequences for their actions.

**Yeoman farmers.** The largest single group of southern whites were family farmers, the **"yeoman"** praised by Thomas Jefferson as the backbone of a free society. On farms of about one hundred acres or less, they raised livestock and grew corn and sweet potatoes for their own consumption, and perhaps tended a little cotton or tobacco to supply much-needed hard currency. The yeoman families lived much more isolated lives than their counterparts in the North and, because of their chronic shortage of cash, lacked many of the amenities that northerners enjoyed. Some southern yeomen, particularly younger men, rented land or hired themselves out as agricultural workers. Small farmers did not own slaves, and their prospect for acquiring enough land or money to do so was nil, but they still supported slavery out of strongly held views of racial superiority and because a large free black population would compete with them for a decent living.

**Poor whites.** The lowest rung on the white social ladder was occupied by people who lived on the most marginal lands in the South—the pine barrens, swamps, and sandy hill country. **Poor whites,** variously called "hillbillies," "white trash," "crackers," or "clay eaters," just barely survived as subsistence farmers, usually as squatters. Their reputed laziness was primarily due to an extremely inadequate diet;

malnutrition left them susceptible to malaria, hookworm, and other diseases that produced lethargy. Slaves sometimes had better physical living conditions than poor whites.

**Free blacks in the South.** Not all African Americans in the South before the Civil War were slaves. More than a quarter million "free persons of color" were concentrated in the states of Maryland, North Carolina, and Virginia as well as the cities of Charleston and New Orleans. Blacks who managed to buy their freedom or were freed by their masters, a practice outlawed throughout the South during the 1830s, occupied a strange place in society. While a handful found financial success, even becoming landowners with slaves of their own, the majority were laborers, farm hands, domestics, factory workers, and craftsmen who never escaped poverty. Religion played an important role in the lives of free blacks, as it did for slaves, and black evangelical churches, particularly Baptist and African Methodist Episcopal (AME), flourished. Perhaps because planters felt sentimental toward children they had sired with slaves, mulattos accounted for a significant percentage of the free persons of color. As a group, mulattos tended to look down on those with darker skin, whether free or slave.

## Slave Society and Culture

The conditions slaves faced depended on the size of the plantation or farm where they worked, the work they had to do, and, of course, the whim of their master. Those who worked the fields with their owner and his family tended to receive better treatment than plantation slaves under an overseer, who was interested only in maximizing the harvest and had no direct investment in their well-being. Household slaves, blacksmiths, carpenters, and **drivers** (slaves responsible for a gang of workers) were better off than field hands. Ultimately, any slave's fate was determined by his or her owner; the use of corporal punishment and the granting of privileges, such as allowing a visit to a nearby plantation, were his decisions alone.

**Labor and subsistence.** Field hands—men, women, and children—might work as long as sixteen hours a day during the harvest and ten or more hours a day in winter; the work week was typically six days long, with Saturday usually a half day. Slaves were organized into gangs of about twenty-five under a driver and overseer (the **gang system**), or individuals were given a specific job to do each day (the **task system**). Punishment was inflicted by the overseer or driver if the assigned job was not completed or done poorly or if equipment was lost or damaged. Usually, punishment meant a whipping, but extra work and a reduction in food rations were other forms of discipline. Consistently good work was rewarded by extra food, a pass to visit friends or family on another plantation, or the privilege of having a vegetable garden.

Ready-made clothes were generally given to men twice a year, and everyone received new shoes about once a year; women were provided with cloth to make dresses for themselves and clothes for their children. Some plantations ran a kitchen for the slaves, but it was more common for food to be distributed weekly to individuals and families. Typically, rations consisted of cornmeal, salt pork or bacon, and molasses. The number of calories was adequate, but the diet had little variety and was heavy on starch and fats. It could be supplemented with fish, small game, chickens, and vegetables from a garden, if the master approved. On large plantations, slave quarters were located near the fields and main house. They were one- or two-room dirt-floored cabins that were hot in summer and extremely cold in winter. More than one family usually lived in a cabin.

The overall slave population was not generally healthy. The combination of hard physical labor, corporal punishment, a diet often lacking nutritional value, and poor living conditions contributed to a very high infant mortality rate—at least 20 percent of the slave children died before the age of five—and a much lower life expectancy than southern whites. While it was in the economic interest of planters to keep their slaves healthy, most did not provide satisfactory medical care. A few large plantations had infirmaries, but conditions in them were often worse than in the slave quarters.

**The slave family.** While without legal standing, slave marriages were accepted by most planters because they believed marriage made slaves easier to control and less likely to run away. The marriage ceremony itself might have consisted of a man and woman **"jumping the broom,"** a custom that affirmed their commitment to each other before the slave community; a formal wedding in the main house with the planter and his family; or just a simple agreement from the owner. A planter or farmer's acceptance of marriage did not mean, however, that he respected the institution. Selling wives away from husbands or children from parents was common, as was the sexual abuse of slave women. Slave children who were sent to another plantation would be taken in by a family belonging to their new owner.

Despite the ever-present threat of having their family torn apart, slaves did their best to maintain stability. The division of responsibility between husband and wife was much the same as in white society: the husband acted as the head of the household and was a provider—fishing and hunting for extra food, collecting firewood, and fixing up the cabin; the wife cared for their children when they were very young and did the cooking, sewing, and any other domestic chores. Many **slave narratives,** accounts of slavery told by the slaves themselves, note how much work women did after they had spent a long day in the field tending cotton. A pregnant woman would work in the fields as long as the overseer believed she could do her job. Mothers would be given time off to nurse a young child who was sick. Beyond mother, father, and children was an extended family of uncles, aunts, and grandparents as well as individuals who had no direct familial ties, all providing a strong support network in the slave community.

**Slave religion and culture.** In much the same way they viewed slave marriage, planters also saw religion as a means of controlling their slaves, and they encouraged it. Slaves, in a prayer house built on the plantation or at services in their master's nearby church, heard time and again a simple sermon—obey your master and do not steal or lie. But the slaves also developed their own religion, often an amalgam of evangelical Christianity and West-African beliefs and practices, and it was the source of a very different message. At services held secretly during the evening in the slave quarters or nearby woods, prayers, songs, and sermons focused on ultimate deliverance from bondage. Not at all surprising was the emphasis on Moses, the "promised land," and the Israelites' release from Egypt in both slave religion and song.

Music, particularly what became known as the "Negro spiritual," was an important part of slave culture. It seemed to southern whites that slaves sang all the time, and apologists for slavery argued that this showed slaves were happy and content with their lot. They evidently ignored the songs' lyrics about the burden of backbreaking labor; sorrow over the breakup of families; and hope for the end to slavery, either in the hereafter or sooner, if escape to the North could be arranged.

## Resistance to and the Defense of Slavery

Resistance to slavery took several forms. Slaves would pretend to be ill, refuse to work, do their jobs poorly, destroy farm equipment, set fire to buildings, and steal food. These were all individual acts rather than part of an organized plan for revolt, but the objective was to upset the routine of the plantation in any way possible. On some plantations, slaves could bring grievances about harsh treatment from an overseer to their master and hope that he would intercede on their behalf. Although many slaves tried to run away, few succeeded for more than a few days, and they often returned on their own. Such escapes were more a protest—a demonstration that it could be done—than a dash for freedom. As advertisements in southern newspapers seeking the return of runaway slaves made clear, the goal of most runaways was to find their wives or children who had been sold to another planter. The fabled **underground railroad,** a series of safe houses for runaways organized by abolitionists and run by former slaves like Harriet Tubman, actually helped only about a thousand slaves reach the North.

**Slave revolts.** The United States had fewer violent slave revolts than the Caribbean colonies and Brazil, and the reasons were largely demographic. In other parts of the Western Hemisphere, the African slave trade had continued, and the largely male slave populations came to significantly outnumber the white masters. In the United States, with the exception of Mississippi and South Carolina, slaves were not in the majority, and whites remained very much in control. Perhaps most important, marriage and family ties, which formed the foundation of the U.S. slave community, worked against a violent response to slavery.

Nevertheless, in the early nineteenth century, there were several major plots for revolt. Gabriel Prosser recruited perhaps as many as a thousand slaves in 1800 with a plan to set fire to Richmond, the capital of Virginia, and take the governor prisoner. The plot failed when other slaves informed the authorities about Prosser. In 1822, Denmark Vesey's scheme to seize Charleston was also betrayed by slaves who were involved in the conspiracy. Despite these failures, some African Americans, most notably David Walker (in his 1829 *Appeal to the Colored Citizens of the World*), still saw armed rebellion as the only appropriate response to slavery.

Motivated by religious visions of racial violence, Nat Turner organized a revolt in Virginia in August 1831. He and a close-knit group of slaves went from farm to farm killing any whites they found; in the end, fifty-five of them were found dead, mostly women and children. Turner intentionally did not try to gain support from slaves on nearby plantations before the short-lived revolt began. He had hoped that the brutality of the murders (the victims were hacked to death or decapitated) would both terrorize slaveowners and gain him recruits. Once he had a larger force, he planned to change tactics: women, children, and any men who did not resist would be spared. But only a few slaves joined Turner, and the militia put down the rebellion after a few days. Turner, who managed to elude capture for several months, was eventually tried and hanged along with nineteen other rebels. Other trials of alleged conspirators in the revolt resulted in the execution of many innocent slaves by enraged whites.

**The debate over slavery in Virginia.** Turner's revolt convinced many Virginians—particularly farmers in the western part of the state who owned few slaves—that it was time to end slavery. Early in 1832, the state legislature considered a proposal for gradual emancipation, with owners compensated for their loss. Although the measure prompted an open debate on the merits of slavery, it failed in both houses, but by only comparatively small margins. Ironically, after coming to the brink of abolishing slavery, Virginia, and then other southern states, moved in the opposite direction and opted for greater control over the black population. New **slave codes** passed in each state increased patrols to locate runaway slaves and guard against new outbreaks of violence, prohibited African Americans from holding meetings, denied free blacks the right to own any kind of weapon, made it illegal to educate a slave (Turner knew how to read and write), and outlawed the **manumission** (freeing) of slaves by their owners.

**In defense of slavery.** The debate in the Virginia legislature coincided with the publication of William Lloyd Garrison's first issue of the *Liberator.* The moral attack that the abolitionists mounted against slavery called for a new defense from the South. Rather than emphasize that slavery was a profitable labor system essential to the health of the southern economy, apologists turned to the Bible and history. They found ample support for slavery in both the Old and New Testaments and pointed out that the great civilizations of the ancient world—Egypt, Greece, and Rome—were slave societies.

The most ludicrous defense of slavery was that enslavement was actually good for African Americans: slaves were happy and content under the paternal care of their master and his family, toward whom they felt a special affection, and talk of liberty and freedom was irrelevant because slaves could not even understand those concepts. The proponents of slavery also maintained that slaves on plantations in the South were better off than the "wage slaves" in northern factories, where business owners had no real investment in their workers. In contrast, planters had every incentive to make sure their slaves were well fed, clothed, and housed. Harsh masters, more often than not, were northerners who had moved to the South, rather than those born and bred in the region, the proponents claimed. Underlying all the arguments was a fundamental belief in the superiority of whites.

Public discussion of slavery and its abolishment effectively ended in the South after 1832; all segments of white society supported slavery, whether they owned slaves or not. The growing isolation of the region was reflected by splits in several Protestant denominations over the slavery question. In 1844, the Methodist Episcopal Church South was established as a separate organization, and a year later, southern Baptists formed their own group, the Southern Baptist Convention. Not only did southerners try to counter the abolitionists in print, they wanted help in suppressing the antislavery movement altogether. In 1835, the South Carolina legislature called on the northern states to make it a crime to publish or distribute anything that might incite a slave revolt. The resolutions made it very clear that South Carolina considered slavery an internal issue and that any attempt to interfere with it would be unlawful and resisted.

**North versus South.** The existence of slavery was just the most visible difference between the North and South. The two regions' economies had been complementary, but by most measures—the number of railroads, canals, factories, and urban centers and the balance between agriculture and industry—they were moving in opposite directions. The reform movements that arose in the decades before the Civil War made few inroads in the South because any calls for social change were associated with abolitionism. Although wealthy planters hired tutors for their children, and many of their sons went on to college, even public education was considered not particularly important in the South.

In the North, the rejection of slavery as an institution did not mean there was widespread support for extending full political rights, let alone social equality, to African Americans. Residents of both the North and South believed in democracy, but at the time, the goal that would attain full democracy for the nation was the expansion of the franchise to all white males. Both northerners and southerners took part in the westward movement of the country, looking for better land and greater opportunities, but they could not escape the divisive issue of slavery. It was over the status of slavery in the new territories of the west that the sectional lines dividing the nation became rigid.

# EXPANSION, WAR, AND SECTIONAL TENSIONS

In the spring of 1803, the western boundary of the United States had reached the Mississippi River, and the original thirteen states had expanded to seventeen with the admission of Vermont (1791), Kentucky (1792), Tennessee (1796), and Ohio (1803). By the end of the year, the size of the country had doubled with the Louisiana Purchase, bringing under American control land stretching from the Gulf of Mexico to British Canada and from the Mississippi River to the Rocky Mountains.

Then, in less than a half century, the map of the United States again changed dramatically through a combination of diplomacy and war. Florida was acquired from Spain in 1819. Nagging questions over the border with Canada were worked out through the **Webster-Ashburton Treaty** (1842), and the long-standing dispute with Great Britain over the Oregon Country was resolved by establishing the forty-ninth parallel as the boundary (1846). Texas, which won its independence from Mexico in 1836, was admitted to the Union in 1845. As a result of war with Mexico (1846–48), almost all of the Southwest, including the remainder of Texas, New Mexico, and California, was ceded to the United States.

## The Mexican Borderlands and Oregon

Mexico faced serious problems after it became independent from Spain in 1821. After a brief flirtation with monarchy, it became a republic, and a succession of presidents wrangled over whether the new nation should be centralist, with a strong government in Mexico City, or federalist, with considerable autonomy given to the provinces. Mexico's northern provinces, from Texas to California, were underpopulated and difficult to defend, so Mexico initially encouraged American settlement and trade. Americans were also attracted to potentially rich farmland in the Oregon Country in the early 1840s. While settlers moved into the Republic of Texas, the opening of the

Oregon Trail marked the beginning of significant migration to the Pacific Northwest as well.

**The settlement of Texas.** In the last days of colonial rule in Mexico, Spain had accepted a proposal from several American entrepreneurs to bring American settlers into Texas; Mexico renewed the agreement in 1825 with the provisions that all newcomers become Mexican citizens and accept Catholicism. Promoters of American settlement (known as *empresarios* by the Mexicans), such as Stephen F. Austin, did their jobs well. As many as twenty thousand Americans, along with a thousand slaves, were living in Texas by 1830, mostly southern farmers who found the land cheap and ideal for growing cotton. The growth of the American population, which quickly overwhelmed the group of roughly five thousand Spanish-speaking Mexicans in Texas (*Tejanos*), led Mexico to reverse its "open-door" policy. The Mexican Congress banned slavery in Texas and prohibited further immigration by American citizens, but settlers, both white and slave, continued to cross the border from the United States. Tensions rose as Americans demanded a greater say in their own affairs.

**Texas's independence.** In 1834, General Antonio Lopez de Santa Anna seized power in Mexico, determined to exercise greater control over Texas. His attempts to enforce his centralist policies there failed, and in 1835, he led his troops north. The American Texans and *Tejanos* responded with a declaration of independence (March 2, 1836), but the first confrontation of the Texas Revolution was a disaster for them. Santa Anna's forces completely wiped out the defenders of the Alamo, a mission on the outskirts of San Antonio. Famed frontiersmen Davy Crockett and Jim Bowie died in the fighting. A few weeks later, Santa Anna ordered the execution of all Texas prisoners captured in the Battle of Goliad. The tide decisively turned when Sam Houston, a former governor of Tennessee who had fought with Andrew Jackson, took command of the Texas army. At the Battle of San Jacinto (April 21, 1836), he surprised the Mexican troops, captured Santa Anna, and forced the general to sign a treaty that recognized

Texas's independence in return for his freedom. Although Santa Anna repudiated the treaty after he was released, as did the Mexican government, Texas had become a sovereign nation.

While refusing to acknowledge Texas's independence, Mexico still simmered over the location of the border. The Mexican government had long maintained that Texas was part of the province of Coahuila, whose northern boundary was the Nueces River. Independent Texans, on the other hand, claimed the two-thousand-mile-long Rio Grande as their southern and western border. The enormous territory north and east of the Rio Grande remained in dispute until 1846.

The Republic of Texas chose Sam Houston as its first president, created a legislature and court system, and received diplomatic recognition from the United States, Great Britain, and France. Most Texans, however, expected and wanted their independence to be short-lived. But the Republic's petition for annexation to the United States was refused in 1837, and Texas did not become a state until 1845.

**New Mexico and California.** In 1821, Mexico opened Santa Fe, one of the oldest European settlements in North America, to U.S. trade. In just a short time, wagon trains carrying American goods were making the long trek from Independence, Missouri, to Santa Fe, along what became known as the **Santa Fe Trail.** While fewer settlers went to New Mexico than to Texas, the commercial ties were profitable, and more important, the establishment of the trail demonstrated that the Great Plains was not a barrier to westward expansion.

Mexico also began to encourage U.S. trade with California, whose ports had been effectively off limits to foreign shipping during the period of Spanish rule (1769–1821). Agents of New England merchants established offices for the purpose of exchanging a wide variety of American-made products for California cattle hides and tallow. Many of the agents married Spanish-speaking Californians, or *Californios,* and converted to Catholicism. The first Americans to reach California overland were fur trappers and traders, such as Jedediah Smith (1826) and James Pattie (1828), who reached the Mexican province by way of Santa Fe. By the 1840s, two main routes were open to settlers—the **Old Spanish Trail** from Santa Fe into southern California and the **California Trail,** an Oregon Trail offshoot that crossed the Sierra Nevada and descended into the Sacramento River Valley. Wealthy *Californios* and a small number of early American settlers acquired vast estates known as *ranchos* after Mexico secularized the lands of the Catholic missions in 1834.

Dissatisfaction with the remote Mexican government grew in California throughout the 1830s. A rapid turnover of provincial governors, most of whom knew little about California, exacerbated the negative feelings. By 1845, a native governor, Pio Pico, who was based in Los Angeles, and the Mexican military commandant in Monterey were battling over power. Under these frustrating conditions, many people in California, including the seven hundred or so Americans there, concluded that it was time for a complete break with Mexico, either through independence or by annexation to the United States.

**The Oregon Country.** American claims to the Oregon Country dated back to Captain Robert Gray's discovery of the Columbia River in 1792 and were reinforced by the expedition of Lewis and Clark to the Pacific (1804–06). The official joint occupation of the territory by the United States and Great Britain worked well until the 1840s, when "Oregon fever" gripped many Americans. Wagon trains, organized in the spring in Independence or St. Joseph, Missouri, transported chiefly young families from the Midwest, who traveled northwest for six months over the Oregon Trail, parts of which had long been in use by trappers and early explorers. These pioneer families traveled along the Platte River, crossed through the South Pass of the Rocky Mountains, and then turned north to follow the Snake and Columbia Rivers to the Willamette Valley. Between 1841 and 1845, an estimated five thousand Americans settled in the Oregon Country, by far the largest number of people to have traveled to the Far West.

## The Politics of Expansion

American politics in the 1820s and 1830s had been dominated by domestic issues: the banks, tariffs, and internal improvements. In the 1840s, foreign policy—"American expansion," more accurately—took center stage. The shift was due in part to the political opportunism of John Tyler, William Henry Harrison's vice president. A former Democrat who had broken with Jackson over nullification, Tyler became president when Harrison died after just a month in office. Tyler really did not support the Whig program; his vetoing of bills that would have reestablished the Bank of the United States and raised tariffs led to the wholesale resignation of his cabinet (except Secretary of State Daniel Webster) and lost him what little support the Whig party had earlier given him.

**Tyler's foreign policy.** Having created so many political enemies with his domestic policy, Tyler turned to foreign affairs. The successful negotiation of the Webster-Ashburton Treaty convinced him to call for the annexation of Texas. Secret negotiations with the Republic of Texas began in 1843, and a treaty to formalize annexation was sent to the Senate in April 1844. Tyler claimed that if the United States did not take Texas, Great Britain would. Despite his arguments, opposition to the treaty was strong from both Whigs and Democrats; many saw the annexation as a plot to scrap the Missouri Compromise and extend slavery, while others feared war with Mexico. The treaty was rejected handily.

Defeat was not the end of the matter, however. The election of Democrat James Polk in November 1844 on an expansionist platform suggested that the public mood had changed. Rather than quickly reintroduce the treaty, which had to be ratified by two thirds of the Senate, Tyler was able to accomplish annexation through a joint resolution of Congress, which required only simple majorities in both houses to pass. The joint resolution was approved and signed by Tyler as one of his last acts in office (March 1, 1845).

**The election of 1844.** The front runners for the presidency in 1844 were Henry Clay for the Whigs and Martin Van Buren for the Democrats. Before the parties' nominating conventions, the two men met and agreed to keep the issues of expansion and slavery out of the campaign. Both men published lengthy letters in the national press opposing the immediate annexation of Texas. Clay easily won the Whig nomination, but the Democrats deadlocked because Van Buren's stand on Texas cost him votes. In the end, he could not hurdle the party's rule that required a candidate to win two thirds of the vote of the convention for nomination. James Polk of Tennessee, a former Speaker of the House, was chosen on the ninth ballot. The Democratic platform called for the "reannexation" of Texas and the "reoccupation" of Oregon; in fact, one of the party's most effective slogans was "Fifty-four Forty or Fight!," a reference to the northernmost boundary of the Oregon Country.

Clay was on the defensive from the beginning, but he eventually came out with a qualified endorsement for the annexation of Texas. His strategy backfired. Whigs in New York had switched to the antislavery Liberty party in enough numbers to cost Clay the state. Had Clay taken New York, he would have won the presidency by seven electoral votes. Only thirty-eight thousand popular votes separated the candidates, but the margin for Polk in the Electoral College was 170 to Clay's 105.

**Settling the Oregon question.** Despite the rhetoric of the presidential campaign, Polk was not ready to go to war with Great Britain over Oregon. Joint occupation, however, was becoming meaningless as more and more American settlers moved into the territory. The practical reality was that Americans far outnumbered the British fur trappers, and the fur trade was in decline in any event. While the British initially rebuffed an American offer to negotiate, both countries ultimately agreed to settle their differences peacefully in 1846. The solution was to extend the Webster-Ashburton Treaty line (the forty-ninth parallel) to the Pacific, making some twists and turns in Puget Sound so that all of Vancouver Island went to Great Britain. That accomplished, Polk remained dissatisfied with his obtaining American control over most of the disputed part of Oregon and his bringing Texas into the Union (December 1845); he wanted New Mexico and California as well and this time was prepared to go to war, if necessary.

**The rise of manifest destiny.** Polk's vision of a country that stretched from the Atlantic to the Pacific was not a new idea, but soon after his election, Americans received a well-phrased rationale to justify expansion. In 1845, John L. O'Sullivan, publisher of the *Democratic Review,* wrote that it was the nation's "manifest destiny to overspread and to possess the whole of the continent which Providence has given us for the development of the great experiment of liberty and federated self-government entrusted to us." The two words "manifest destiny" quickly caught on, soon coming to mean that those who favored expansion had God on their side and were engaged in the noble task of spreading democracy. Despite the fact that the expansionist doctrine was based partly on the notion of racial superiority—O'Sullivan referred to the "superior vigor of the Anglo-Saxon race"—it appealed both to supporters of slavery, who wanted Texas annexed, and to antislavery advocates, who favored adding California and Oregon to the Union.

Proponents of manifest destiny claimed that a continental United States would benefit from trade with Asia, from the commercial advantages of San Francisco Bay and Puget Sound, and from lower tariffs. Sea-to-sea expansion would also safeguard democracy, give the nation room to grow, and preserve the essential character of the country as an agricultural nation in the Jeffersonian tradition.

## The War with Mexico

When Congress approved the annexation of the Republic of Texas, Mexico broke off diplomatic relations with the United States. Polk responded by ordering U.S. troops under the command of General Zachary Taylor into the new American state. He also sent his personal emissary, John Slidell, to Mexico City with a proposal to purchase New Mexico and California and fix the boundary of Texas at the Rio Grande. By March 1846, however, the Mexican government had been overthrown, the new Mexican president had reaffirmed Mexico's claims to all of Texas, Slidell's mission had failed, and Taylor's forces had advanced to the Rio Grande. Fighting began around Matamoros in April. When the news reached Washington a month later, Polk did not hesitate to send a war message to Congress, stating "Mexico has ... shed American blood on American soil." The fact that hostilities had broken out in still-disputed territory was not considered particularly relevant. President Polk signed the declaration of war against Mexico on May 13, 1846.

**The war in California and New Mexico.** If Texas provided the spark for war, California provided the motive. The United States had long been interested in California, primarily because San Francisco had the finest natural harbor on the Pacific coast. In 1842, American naval forces, mistakenly believing that war had broken out between the United States and Mexico, landed at Monterey. Polk had confidential agents in place by 1844 to encourage American settlers in California to push for either annexation or independence under U.S. protection. On June 14, 1846, a small group of Americans in the Sacramento Valley ran a homemade flag up a pole and declared California an independent nation. The so-called **Bear Flag Revolt,** which was supported by Captain John C. Frémont, was short-lived. When the Mexican War actually did begin, Polk lost little time in sending the Pacific fleet under Commodore John Sloat to California, with orders to claim the province as occupied territory. Sloat landed at Monterey in early July and declared California part of the United States. Mexican resistance to the American takeover was over by January 1847. Virtually no fighting took place in New Mexico. Colonel Stephen Kearny arrived in Santa Fe in August 1846 with the "Army of the West," a force of about seventeen hundred men, and simply proclaimed that New Mexico was new American territory. He established a temporary territorial government before moving on to California.

**The war in Mexico.** Polk had achieved his most important expansionist goals by the summer of 1846, but fighting with Mexico continued for another two years. Taylor won important battles at Palo Alto and Monterrey in northern Mexico, making him a national hero. President Polk agreed to let Santa Anna, then in exile in Cuba, back into Mexico only if he promised to help negotiate a settlement. Santa Anna instead took command of the government and pledged continued resistance against the American invasion. Severely outnumbered, Santa Anna's forces were defeated by Taylor's troops at the Battle of Buena Vista (February 1847). The main theater of the war then shifted to the heart of Mexico. General Winfield Scott landed near Veracruz on March 29 and spent the spring and summer pressing the campaign toward Mexico City. The fall of the Mexican capital in September ended the war.

**The Treaty of Guadalupe Hidalgo.** Nicholas Trist, an official in the State Department, opened negotiations with Mexico in January 1848. The resulting Treaty of Guadalupe Hidalgo was ratified by Mexico in February and by the Senate in March. Under its terms, Mexico relinquished all claims to Texas north of the Rio Grande and ceded New Mexico and California to the United States. The lands of the **Mexican Cession** also encompassed Nevada, Utah, most of Arizona, and parts of Colorado and Wyoming. The United States agreed to pay $15 million for the new territory and an additional $3 million to assume the debt owed by Mexico to American citizens for past claims.

## Slavery in the New Lands

With the Mexican War, the extension of slavery into the territories became a national issue, and several solutions to the problem were suggested. Shortly after the fighting began, Democrat David Wilmot of Pennsylvania introduced an amendment to an appropriation bill in the House of Representatives calling for the prohibition of slavery in any territory to be acquired from Mexico. Although the **Wilmot Proviso** never became law, John C. Calhoun responded to it with a series of resolutions, maintaining that any attempt to ban slavery was unconstitutional: slaves were property, and if a person wanted to take his property to another part of the country, no law could prevent him from doing so. Furthermore, the Fifth Amendment prevented Congress from depriving anyone of their property without due process. On middle ground between these two extreme positions was a proposal for **"squatter sovereignty"** (later known as **"popular sovereignty"**), championed by Lewis Cass of Michigan. Popular sovereignty, if accepted, would let the settlers themselves decide whether slavery would be allowed in their territory.

**The election of 1848.** With his foreign policy objectives achieved, Polk decided not to run for a second term. Zachary Taylor was the nominee of the Whigs. Although himself a slaveowner, he had not taken a public stand on slavery or any other major issue of the day and, in fact, had never voted in a national election. The Whigs had no party platform and ran the campaign solely on Taylor's war record. The Democrats chose Lewis Cass, but their platform called on Congress not to interfere with slavery and did not mention popular sovereignty. The wild card in the election was the **Free-Soil party,** a coalition of three groups: dissident Democrats who supported the Wilmot Proviso, members of the abolitionist Liberty party, and antislavery Whigs from New England.

The major parties ran a distinctly sectional campaign. In the North, the Whigs claimed that Taylor would back the Wilmot Proviso if Congress approved it, while they reminded southern voters that their candidate was a son of the South. The Democrats assured both parts of the country that the territories would decide the slavery question on their own without Congress, leaving northerners to believe that the West would be free and southerners confident that slaves would be allowed. The results of the election showed the effects of the campaign. Taylor won the presidency with 163 electoral votes (eight slave and seven free states) to Cass's 127 (seven slave and eight free states); the Free-Soil party did not win any states but did split the vote in New York to Taylor's favor and the Ohio vote in Cass's.

**The California gold rush.** In January 1848, gold was discovered in California. The news spread around the world and was confirmed by President Polk in his annual message to Congress in December. Tens of thousands of people, mostly white Americans, flooded into California, looking to make their fortune in the gold fields; a polyglot mix of free African Americans, Mexicans, Pacific Islanders, and Europeans rushed in as well. With the influx of the **forty-niners,** who were chiefly young men without families, the population of California reached one hundred thousand by the end of 1849 and continued to grow. Easy-to-locate gold deposits were soon played out, and by 1852, many miners found themselves wage earners for highly mechanized and well-financed mining operations. Others gave up prospecting soon after they arrived in California, realizing that more money could be made in providing food, lodging, and other services to the new arrivals.

The economic and social impact of the gold rush was less important at the time than California's political future. A state constitution that prohibited slavery was adopted in the fall of 1849, and in December, President Taylor recommended that California be admitted into the Union. Admission was a volatile issue because the numbers of slave and free states were balanced at fifteen each. Oregon had been organized as a free territory in 1848 on the basis of its provisional constitution and the fact that it lay north of the line established by the Missouri Compromise of 1820. Extending that line—36°30′ north latitude—to the Pacific would have cut California in two. It fell to Congress, which had scrupulously tried to avoid the slavery question for almost three decades, to decide slavery's fate in California and the rest of the Mexican Cession.

The decade preceding the Civil War began positively with a compromise that seemed to settle the several outstanding issues of the Mexican Cession. Despite lawmakers' efforts, however, slavery remained a burning national question; new political alignments were formed that reflected the division of the country between North and South, and the creation of new territories raised anew the problem of the extension of slavery. Court decisions and popular literature hardened the feelings of both proslavery and antislavery individuals. In the end, the nation could not overcome the fundamental divisions over slavery and states' rights, and the Union was dissolved.

## The Compromise of 1850

With California ready for statehood in 1850, a solution to the problem of the extension of slavery raised by the Mexican Cession could no longer be delayed. Although President Taylor was the titular head of the Whigs, he had little political clout. The Whigs turned to Henry Clay, who was responsible for the Missouri Compromise of 1820 and the settlement of the nullification controversy in the 1830s, to devise yet another compromise that would satisfy all factions.

**Clay's omnibus bill.** Clay knew that the issues dividing the country went beyond the lands acquired from the war with Mexico. Many northerners were concerned about slaves still being bought and sold in the nation's capital, while southerners wanted a more effective means than the 1793 fugitive slave law for recapturing their runaway slaves. In January 1850, Clay presented a series of resolutions known as the **omnibus bill,** which addressed all the outstanding questions. According to the bill, California would be admitted to the Union as a free state; New Mexico and Utah would be organized as territories with the status of slavery to be decided by popular sovereignty; the slave trade, but not slavery itself, would be terminated in the District of Columbia; the fugitive slave law would be strengthened; Congress would declare that it had no right to interfere in the interstate slave trade; the disputed boundary between Texas and New Mexico would be adjusted; and the United States would assume the pre-annexation debt of Texas.

**The politics of compromise.** The debate in the Senate on the omnibus bill stretched out for six months amid talk of the southern states' seceding from the Union. Clay made an eloquent defense of his proposed settlement on the Senate floor, strongly emphasizing that secession would lead only to war. Calhoun, too ill to deliver his response to Clay's speech, listened as a colleague read it for him. He called for equal rights for the South in the territories, an end to attacks against slavery, and a constitutional amendment that would, in some vaguely described manner, restore power to the southern states. Daniel Webster spoke in support of the compromise and criticized extremists on both sides of the issues—abolitionists as well as the vocal defenders of slavery. He argued that the climate and soil of the territories precluded the extension of slavery there. Senator William H. Seward of New York condemned Clay's resolutions on the grounds that any compromise with slavery was wrong.

The omnibus bill failed because all of the measures had to be voted on as a package. Senator Stephen Douglas, a Democrat from Illinois, rescued the compromise by pushing through five separate bills, each of which independently drew enough support to pass. In addition to admitting California as a free state, the **Compromise of 1850** included the following four pieces of legislation: the **Texas and New Mexico Act,** under which New Mexico became a territory without restrictions on slavery (that is, the matter was to be settled by popular sovereignty) and the boundary between Texas and New Mexico was settled, with the United States paying Texas $10 million to relinquish all its territorial claims; the **Utah Act,** which established Utah as a territory under the same terms as New Mexico regarding slavery; an amendment to the **Fugitive Slave Act,** which put all cases involving runaway slaves under federal jurisdiction in a manner that clearly favored slaveowners; and the **Act Abolishing the Slave Trade in the District of Columbia,** which did exactly what its title indicates—it abolished commerce in slaves in the capital city, effective January 1, 1851, with the further provision that the District of Columbia could not be used as a shipping point for the purpose of sale.

**The Fugitive Slave Act of 1850.** Although the running away of slaves was never a serious problem, the new fugitive slave law was the one major victory the South won from the Compromise of 1850; it was also the most controversial. Special commissioners were appointed to hear cases regarding fugitives and could issue warrants for the arrest of runaway slaves; the commissioners received ten dollars for every alleged runaway returned to his or her owner but only five dollars if it was determined that the slave should not be returned. Slaves who claimed to be free were not permitted to testify in their own defense and did not have recourse to a jury trial. Anyone who interfered with the capture of fugitive slaves faced heavy fines, and obstructing the return of a slave was punishable by fines, imprisonment, and civil liabilities. Despite the law's enforcement provisions, several northern states enacted **personal liberty laws,** which prohibited officials from aiding in the recovery of fugitive slaves. Occasionally, violence broke out when a crowd of abolitionists tried to "rescue" slaves who were about to be brought before commissioners. The refusal of many northerners to cooperate with agents exercising their rights under the law made the Fugitive Slave Act a dead letter as soon as it was enacted.

**The impact of *Uncle Tom's Cabin.*** Northern views of slavery hardened after the publication of Harriet Beecher Stowe's sentimental novel *Uncle Tom's Cabin,* in which she wrote about the injustice of the institution in reaction to the Fugitive Slave Act of 1850. The daughter of the noted preacher Lyman Beecher and sister of Reverend Henry Ward Beecher, Stowe first serialized *Uncle Tom's Cabin* in an abolitionist magazine in 1851. The story appeared as a book the following year. The novel dramatically portrays the terror of the slave

Eliza as she runs across ice floes on the Ohio River, clutching her tiny baby, and the nobility of Uncle Tom as he is whipped to death by Simon Legree. The book makes it clear that the concept of slavery is inherently evil; although Tom had been owned by a "kindly master" before he was sold to Legree, it was the institution itself that led to families being torn apart.

Stowe's novel was an immediate success, selling two million copies by the end of 1852 and waking a mass audience to the harshness of slavery. The impact of *Uncle Tom's Cabin* is difficult to overestimate. According to Stowe's son, when President Lincoln met Mrs. Stowe at a White House affair, he is alleged to have remarked, "So this is the little lady who started the Civil War." The story is probably apocryphal, but it makes the point that northern views on slavery indeed changed after the publication of her novel.

## Political Realignment in the 1850s

The presidential election of 1852 marked the beginning of the end of the Whig party. With its northern and southern wings divided over the Fugitive Slave Law, the best the party could do was nominate another hero of the Mexican War, General Winfield Scott. The Democrats turned away from Millard Fillmore, Taylor's vice president, who had succeeded to the presidency upon Taylor's death in 1850, and chose Franklin Pierce of New Hampshire as their candidate. Although both parties supported the Compromise of 1850, the Democrats were able to better overcome their internal differences, and Pierce won a landslide victory in the Electoral College, 254 to 42. The Whigs never recovered from the defeat.

The election of 1852 was an important watershed. As the Whig party fell apart, Americans formed new political alignments. Southern Whigs moved into the Democratic party, while northern Whigs joined the new Republican party, formed in 1855. In addition, another party—the **American party** (also known as the **Know-Nothings**)—attracted anti-immigration nativists, opponents of the extension of slavery, and voters disillusioned with the performance of both the Whigs and Democrats. The year 1852 also marked the last election for eighty years in which candidates from both parties collected popular and electoral votes from throughout the country; party affiliation and voter support remained largely sectional until the election of Franklin Roosevelt in 1932.

**The Kansas-Nebraska Act.** The Compromise of 1850 did not address the issue of slavery in the large unorganized territory in the Great Plains, but with California clamoring for the construction of a transcontinental railroad link to the East, the issue had to be addressed. Senator Douglas, who favored a northern rail route to California that would benefit Chicago, was the author of the **Kansas-Nebraska Act.** It created two territories—Kansas and Nebraska—and declared the Missouri Compromise null and void; the matter of slavery in the new territories would be decided by popular sovereignty. Personally, Douglas assumed that Nebraska would become a free state and that Kansas would allow slavery.

The Kansas-Nebraska Act created far more problems than it purported to solve. Antislavery northerners, who held the Missouri Compromise sacrosanct, thought the legislation sold Kansas into slavery, and they condemned Douglas for being a dupe of southern interests. Their suspicions gained credibility with the ratification of the **Gadsden Purchase** at the end of 1853. President Pierce had sent James Gadsden, a railroad expert who happened to be a southerner, to Mexico to negotiate the purchase of the Mesilla Valley, the area south of the Gila River in present-day Arizona. An army survey had indicated this region to be a feasible route for a southerly transcontinental railroad, which had considerable support in the South. The treaty originally included Baja California, but opposition from free-soilers limited the purchase to the land that makes up the southern borders of Arizona and New Mexico today. The purchase completed the continental expansion of the United States.

**"Bleeding Kansas."** Senator Douglas did not anticipate the violence that would accompany the creation of the Kansas Territory, as both proslavery and antislavery settlers rushed in to gain control of the government. Competing territorial legislatures were established in 1855, and the free-state force drafted a constitution prohibiting not only slavery but also the settling of free blacks in Kansas. On May 21, 1856, a proslavery mob attacked the free-state stronghold at Lawrence, burning buildings and destroying property. John Brown, a militant abolitionist, and a small band of supporters retaliated by killing five men at Pottawatomie Creek a few days later. Violence erupted in the U.S. Senate over Kansas as well. Charles Sumner of Massachusetts condemned southerners for their actions in Kansas in extremely strong language. Preston Brooks, a congressman from South Carolina, decided to punish Sumner for his insults and beat him with his cane in a confrontation in the Senate chamber. Onlookers from the South did nothing to help Sumner.

**The election of 1856.** The new Republican party chose Californian John C. Frémont, explorer and military leader, as its presidential candidate in 1856. The party's platform, which condemned the repeal of the Missouri Compromise and called for free soil, was more important than the nominee; the Republicans were the first major political party to take a position on slavery. James Buchanan, an experienced politician and diplomat who had served in both the House and Senate and had been secretary of state in the Polk administration, was the Democratic candidate. He ran on a platform that endorsed the Kansas-Nebraska Act and congressional noninterference in slavery. The American party turned to former president Millard Fillmore.

The Republicans recognized that they had no chance of winning in the slave states, so there were in effect two sectional campaigns: Frémont against Buchanan in the North and Buchanan against Fillmore in the South. The American party's anti-Catholic and anti-immigrant stand cost it dearly. The Democrats swept the South with the exception of the border states of Maryland and Delaware and also showed strength in key northern states, where their attacks against nativism and calls for religious freedom gained the party support from ethnic voters. Frémont won eleven of the sixteen free states and came close to winning the election without any backing at all in the South, which was significant because it showed that a party with an antislavery platform and an exclusively northern base could win the presidency.

## The Union in Crisis

Buchanan won, but his term in office began inauspiciously. Two days after his inauguration, the Supreme Court handed down its long-awaited decision in *Dred Scott* v. *Sanford,* a key case that addressed the status of African Americans in American society. The ruling of Chief Justice Roger Taney was hailed in the South but blasted by infuriated antislavery forces in the North. The decision further heightened the sectional tensions in the country.

**The Dred Scott decision.** As a slave, Dred Scott had been taken by his master from the slave state of Missouri to the free state of Illinois and then to the free territory of Wisconsin, where they lived during the 1830s. After his master died, Scott tried to buy his freedom; when that failed, he sought relief in the courts. He claimed that although he had been brought back to Missouri, his past residence in a free state and territory had made him a free person.

Taney's decision effectively rejected Scott's claim from the outset. He stated that Scott was a slave, not a citizen of either the United States or Missouri, and therefore had no right to bring suit in the federal courts. Taney put forward a racial justification for denying blacks, free or slave, the rights of citizenship. From the time the Constitution was ratified, African Americans were "regarded as beings of an inferior order, and altogether unfit to associate with the white race, either in social or political relations." Further, Taney declared that the Missouri Compromise, which had created the concept of free and slave states based on geography, had been unconstitutional from its inception because it violated the Fifth Amendment's protection of property.

In his view, slaves were nothing more than property, as southerners had always asserted they were.

The *Dred Scott* decision astonished antislavery northerners, who took their wrath out on Buchanan. Even though the president had not appointed the Taney Court and had no influence on its decision, he was seen as another puppet of the slaveowners. The fact that Buchanan was one of the signatories of the **Ostend Manifesto** (1854), which threatened an American takeover of Cuba after Spain had spurned an offer from the United States to buy the colony, seemed to give additional credence to this view. It was widely believed that the South was interested in acquiring Cuba to make it a slave state.

**More trouble in Kansas.** Despite his political troubles, Buchanan hoped to bring about a solution to the tensions in Kansas between the rival territorial governments. He suggested that an elected territorial convention create a constitution either permitting or prohibiting slavery and that Congress, after reviewing the document, vote on admitting Kansas as a state. The president failed to take into account the numerous instances of voting fraud in the territory's brief history. Although in the majority, free-staters boycotted the election for the convention, and the proslavery delegates left in control drafted a constitution that permitted slavery. Through a territorial referendum limited to just the constitution's slavery provisions, also boycotted by the antislavery forces, the **Lecompton Constitution** was approved. The free-state legislature called for another vote on the constitution, and the result was overwhelmingly negative. Although a proponent of popular sovereignty, Buchanan endorsed the Lecompton Constitution anyway as a way of paying back his southern supporters and tried to get Kansas admitted to the Union as a slave state. Congress, however, ordered yet another closely supervised election, and the voters rejected the Lecompton Constitution for a second time. With that vote, Kansas was no longer a burning issue in national politics. Buchanan's inept handling of the Kansas constitution succeeded only in alienating northern Democrats.

**The Panic of 1857.** An economic downturn in late 1857 hurt business conditions. California gold had inflated the nation's currency, and speculators had overly promoted railroads and real estate. Unemployment rose, and grain prices fell because of oversupply, but cotton prices dipped and then quickly recovered. The fact that the South weathered the depression much better than the North was taken by southerners as an important sign of the strength of the southern economy. The more radical individuals in the region, who were seriously considering secession, believed that the South could function independently of the North on cotton exports alone. Northern business interests blamed their problems squarely on Democratic policies, particularly the Tariff of 1857, which had lowered rates significantly. The panic gave the Republicans powerful ammunition for the upcoming presidential election: protective tariffs for business and liberal land laws for encouraging the creation of family farms.

**The Lincoln-Douglas debates.** Senator Douglas had broken with Buchanan over the Lecompton Constitution and was a likely challenge to him for the Democratic nomination in 1860. In Douglas's crucial 1858 Senate reelection campaign, his Republican opponent was Abraham Lincoln, who had been long involved in first Whig and then Republican party politics but had little personal national experience. The debates between the two candidates revolved around their position on slavery. Although Lincoln favored limiting slavery to the states where it already existed and accepted that race made social and political equality for blacks impossible, Douglas was able to portray him as an abolitionist for all intents and purposes. When Douglas was asked how he could reconcile popular sovereignty with the *Dred Scott* decision, the best he could come up with was a weak argument that voters in a territory could reject laws that protected slaves as property. This concept became known as the **Freeport Doctrine,** after the town where the particular debate took place. Although Lincoln lost the election, he did become a national figure, popular in the North but hated in the South.

**The Harpers Ferry incident.** As the decade drew to a close, the North and South grew increasingly polarized. It became difficult to distinguish among those who wanted to abolish slavery immediately, those who simply opposed slavery, and those who were just against the extension of slavery. To southerners, particularly the more radical, anything less than unconditional acceptance of slavery was intolerable. The time for reasoned debate was quickly passing, and critical events escalated the tension.

In October 1859, the fiery John Brown, who had already gained national notoriety for his actions in Kansas, raided the federal arsenal at Harpers Ferry, Virginia, with the apparent objective of fomenting a slave revolt. Federal troops captured Brown and his small band; tried for and convicted of treason, he was hanged on December 2. Southerners soon learned that Brown had connections with prominent abolitionists. While many northerners hailed him as a martyr to the cause of freedom, southerners concluded that the raid on Harpers Ferry was not an isolated incident but part of a conspiracy to mobilize slaves in a mass insurrection. Feeling that their entire way of life was under imminent attack, some southerners looked to **secession**— leaving the Union—as the only solution. The outcome of the upcoming presidential election would be crucial.

**The election of 1860.** To counteract the image of the Republican party as the party of the abolitionists, the Republicans broadened their program to include a protective tariff, free 160-acre homesteads from the public domain, and a more moderate stand on slavery. New York's William Seward, long known for his abolitionist views, was too radical a candidate; therefore, the Republicans nominated Lincoln.

The Democratic party, faced with the challenge of choosing someone who could appeal to all their factions, split in two. The Democrats' convention was in Charleston, South Carolina, the home of the late Calhoun and a hot bed of radical southern sentiment since the 1820s. A platform plank endorsing popular sovereignty was adopted, which prompted the delegates from the Deep South to bolt the convention; the remaining delegates could not agree on a nominee. The Democrats then moved to Baltimore and eventually selected

Stephen Douglas for their candidate—the decision that split the party. Southern Democrats, who wanted federal protection of slavery in the territories, opted to run their own candidate, Buchanan's vice president, John C. Breckinridge of Kentucky. Meanwhile, a group of southern moderates joined with former northern Whigs to form the **Constitutional Union party,** and they chose John Bell, a Tennessee slaveowner who had opposed the Lecompton Constitution, for their candidate.

With the Democratic party divided, Lincoln's election was effectively guaranteed. Although Douglas did relatively well in the popular vote, Lincoln won every state north of the Mason-Dixon Line, along with California and Oregon. The Deep South, from North Carolina to Texas, went to Breckinridge, while Bell took Virginia, Kentucky, and his home state of Tennessee.

**From secession to Fort Sumter.** Lincoln's election was the signal for secession. Not surprising, South Carolina left first (December 20, 1860), followed by Mississippi, Florida, Alabama, Georgia, Louisiana, and Texas. Representatives of the seven states met in Montgomery, Alabama, in February 1861 to form the **Confederate States of America,** draft a new constitution, and elect Jefferson Davis of Mississippi as their first president. Last-minute efforts to compromise failed. Senator John Crittenden of Kentucky tried to work out an arrangement whereby owners of runaway slaves would be compensated for their loss and to amend the Constitution to bar the federal government from interfering with slavery in the South, but events had moved beyond compromise, and the Republicans rejected Crittenden's proposals in any event.

The crucial issue was no longer slavery but whether the southern states would be allowed to secede. By the time Lincoln took office in March, the Confederacy had already commandeered federal arsenals, post offices, government buildings and offices, and most military installations within its territory. Fort Sumter, located on an island in Charleston Harbor, was still in the hands of the United States. Buchanan had tried to send reinforcements and supplies to the fort but backed off when the relief ship was fired upon from the mainland shore. Lincoln tried another approach, announcing that he was sending in just food and medical supplies, not additional troops or ammunition. The South could not abide a continued Union presence in Charleston, and early on April 12, 1861, Confederate artillery opened fire on Fort Sumter. The U.S. forces surrendered the next day. The South had fired the first shot, and Lincoln called for seventy-five thousand volunteers to suppress the insurrection. Virginia, North Carolina, Arkansas, and Tennessee joined the Confederacy during the next month. The Civil War had begun.

At the beginning of the Civil War, the goal of the North was simply to restore the Union. In his first inaugural address (March 4, 1861), President Abraham Lincoln made it very clear that he had no intention of interfering with slavery where it already existed. This point was reiterated in resolutions adopted by Congress in July that stated the war was not waged against "the established institutions" of the southern states. As the conflict dragged on, however, the president realized that the slavery issue could not be avoided—for political, military, and moral reasons. By 1863, the purpose of the war had broadened into a crusade against slavery. Southern leaders fought the war under the dual banners of states' rights and preserving their way of life. Although the overwhelming majority of southerners did not own slaves, support for slavery was widespread, and southerners were deeply concerned about what would happen if it was abolished. The fact that almost all the fighting took place in the South meant that southerners defended their homes against an invading army throughout the Civil War.

## The Balance of Forces

The North had clear advantages over the South at the start of the war. While the South's population was just nine million (more than three million of which were slaves), more than twenty-two million people lived in the northern and border states. The North had the resources and manpower to equip and put many more men in the field than the South and was comparatively an industrial powerhouse, far outstripping the Confederacy in available raw materials, factory production, and railroads. Despite these strengths, the North did face problems, and the South was not as weak as it initially appeared.

**The problems of the North.** That Lincoln won the presidency in 1860 with only forty percent of the popular vote indicated that he did not start his term with an overwhelming political mandate. His own party was divided into Moderates and Radicals; the latter favored immediate emancipation and tried to interfere with his method of conducting the war. The Democratic party in the North, while generally supportive of the administration, contained a peace faction known as the **Copperheads;** their loyalty to the Union was doubted. Militarily, the North faced the difficult challenges of invading a large territory, maintaining long supply lines, and dealing with hostile southern civilians, all of which made its numerical superiority less effective. Northern generals proved less daring and innovative than their southern counterparts, particularly during the early stages of the war.

**Advantages and expectations in the South.** The South intended to fight a mainly defensive war, which meant it needed fewer troops than the invading army. With slaves working either on the farms or in Confederate labor battalions, more white soldiers were available for combat duty than would have been without slavery. Southern strategy, formed from an assumption that support for the war in the North was weak, was to wear down the Union forces until Lincoln was ready to accept the independence of the Confederacy. The South also had a greater number of experienced military commanders than the North; many U.S. army officers, including veterans of the Mexican War, resigned their commissions to fight on the Confederate side when the hostilities broke out. Southerners knew that their economy was not self-sufficient, particularly in wartime, but they anticipated outside help. They fully expected the dependence of Great Britain and France on cotton imports to lead to diplomatic recognition and direct material aid.

## Fighting the War

Everyone expected a short war. Indeed, Lincoln's first call for volunteers required just a ninety-day enlistment. After the First Battle of

Bull Run (July 1861), the hope for a quick victory faded, and the Union implemented the **Anaconda Plan.** Named for the South American constrictor, it was intended to slowly crush the South with a naval blockade of the Atlantic and Gulf coasts and an invasion along the Cumberland, Tennessee, and Mississippi rivers to slice the Confederacy in half. The defense of Washington, D.C., and pressure on the Confederate capital at Richmond were also part of the northern strategy. Jefferson Davis's defensive strategy took advantage of fighting on familiar territory and keeping his army close to the bases of supply. The South was prepared to go on the offensive and move into the North through Maryland and Pennsylvania, however, if opportunities presented themselves.

**The war in the East.** The first major engagement of the war was a disaster for the North. At the First Battle of Bull Run in Virginia, thirty thousand Union troops were routed by a smaller Confederate force as politicians and their families from Washington picnicked on the hills above the battlefield. The defeat prompted Lincoln to put General George McClellan in command of the Army of the Potomac. McClellan spent the next nine months transforming his men into well-trained and disciplined soldiers but then seemed reluctant to let them fight. The army suffered another defeat when it finally did go into the field during the Peninsula Campaign (March–July 1862), an attempt to take Richmond by sea. In September, the South went on the offensive. The Army of Northern Virginia under Robert E. Lee moved into Maryland and met the Union troops at the Battle of Antietam. The bloodiest confrontation of the war ended inconclusively but for the fact that Lee's retreat allowed McClellan to claim victory. Antietam was significant because the outcome finally gave Lincoln the opportunity to issue the **Emancipation Proclamation,** which probably ended any chance the South had of getting Great Britain and France to intervene. Also significant was Lincoln's dismissal of McClellan following his failure to pursue Lee's retreating army; the commander in chief and the general became bitter political rivals.

Lincoln first replaced McClellan with General Ambrose Burnside. Burnside's doubts about his own ability to lead a large army proved correct, and he lost a major battle against Lee and Lieutenant General "Stonewall" Jackson at Fredericksburg in December 1862. The president then turned to General "Fighting Joe" Hooker. Despite Hooker's overwhelming numerical superiority on the battlefield— about one hundred thirty thousand Union troops against sixty thousand southern troops under Lee and Jackson—he was unable to prevent a major Confederate victory at Chancellorsville (May 1863).

**The war in the West.** The Union army had greater success in the West. After driving Confederate forces out of Kentucky, Ulysses S. Grant moved into Tennessee, where he narrowly averted defeat at Shiloh (April 1862), and then proceeded to the Mississippi River, where he captured Memphis (June 1862). Grant's troops moved downriver to lay siege to the important river town of Vicksburg, which held out until July 1863. The navy, under Admiral David Farragut, played an important role in the western campaign, taking New Orleans and then Baton Rouge in May 1862. During the siege of Vicksburg, however, fighting in the West became a stalemate.

Farragut's successes on the Mississippi River were not the only significant naval engagements of the war. The Confederates salvaged the *Merrimack,* a scuttled Union warship in the Norfolk navy yard, reinforced it with iron sheathing, and renamed it the *Virginia.* The ironclad *Virginia* sailed the short distance to Hampton Roads, where it sank several wooden-sided Union ships on blockade duty. The North hastily built its own ironclad, the *Monitor,* an odd vessel that one observer said resembled a "cheese box on a raft." The *Monitor* and the *Virginia* clashed on March 9, 1862. Cannon balls bounced off their iron sides, and neither ship could sink the other. The lesson was clear: future navies would turn to steam-powered, ironclad battleships.

**The war and diplomacy.** The South recognized early that support from other countries could well be decisive in determining the outcome of the war. In Great Britain, public opinion was divided. Merchants and mill owners backed the Confederacy because it was the major supplier of cotton for British textiles mills, but there was also widespread opposition to slavery and the slave trade. Early in the war, relations between the United States and Great Britain soured over the **Trent Affair.** The British steamer *Trent* was stopped by the U.S. navy, and two Confederate diplomats en route to England to seek recognition for the South were taken off. When the British demanded their release on grounds of diplomatic immunity, Lincoln ordered them set free. The British as well as the French built ships for the South, the most notoriously destructive of which was the English-built *Alabama,* but U.S. threats of war forced both countries to back off. Although the foreign-built ships were helpful to the Confederacy, they did not alter the outcome of the war.

France took advantage of the Civil War to pursue its own agenda in the Western Hemisphere. Using alleged unpaid debts as a pretext for intervention, French troops invaded Mexico in 1863 and installed Maximilian of Austria as the "Emperor of Mexico." The United States could do nothing about this blatant violation of the Monroe Doctrine during the war, but it came to the aid of Mexico's legitimate president, Benito Juárez, by moving fifty thousand troops to the border in 1866. France withdrew its forces, and Maximilian ended up in front of a Mexican firing squad.

**The war and manpower.** Although the majority of soldiers on both sides during the Civil War were volunteers, the Confederacy and Union did resort to the draft as the fighting expanded. Conscription of men between the ages of eighteen and thirty-five (the range was later extended to include men aged seventeen to fifty) for a three-year period became law in the South in April 1862. Planters with twenty or more slaves and men employed in what were considered to be essential civilian jobs were exempt. Military service could also be avoided by finding a substitute or simply paying five hundred dollars to the government. The draft in the North was instituted about a year later (March 1863) for men between the ages of twenty and forty-five, and it too included provisions for substitution and payment (three hundred dollars). In July 1863 in New York City, mobs made up largely of Irish immigrants rioted against the Union conscription law and took out their anger on African Americans, whom they blamed for the war. The exemptions and the ability of the wealthy to buy their way out of service caused dissension as troops began to see the conflict as "a rich man's war and a poor man's fight." The percentage of draftees in the Confederate troops was considerably higher than the percentage in the Union army.

## Emancipation

Early in the war, to keep the border states in the Union, Lincoln resisted the demands of the Radical Republicans to free the slaves. Military commanders, though, sometimes took action counter to Lincoln's policy during actual fighting. For example, faced with slaves who had run away to Union lines, General B. F. Butler treated them as contraband and did not return them to their owners (May 1861). General John C. Frémont, in charge of the Department of the West, which included Missouri and Kansas, confiscated the property of rebels and declared their slaves emancipated (August 1861). Lincoln effectively countermanded Frémont's order. Congress, meanwhile, enacted measures that whittled away at slavery. The Confiscation Act of 1861 allowed captured or runaway slaves who had been in use by the Confederacy to support the Union effort instead. Slavery was abolished in the District of Columbia with compensation in April 1862 and in the territories in June 1862. The Second Confiscation Act (July 1862) gave real freedom to slaves belonging to anyone actively participating in the war against the Union.

**Lincoln and gradual emancipation.** Lincoln proposed a plan for gradual emancipation that was by definition a long-term solution to the slavery problem. The plan was aimed at pacifying the slave states that remained in the Union. Lincoln outlined his ideas on several occasions between 1861 and 1862, the fullest statement coming in his Second Message to Congress in December 1862. He urged the House and Senate to adopt a constitutional amendment under which states that abolished slavery by 1900 would be compensated by the federal government. Runaway-slave owners who remained loyal to the United States would also be compensated for their losses. The amendment authorized Congress to appropriate funds to resettle free blacks, if they consented, outside of the country. Although Lincoln himself did not think resettlement was necessary, the idea addressed the deep racial prejudice existing in the country as a whole and particularly white fears about competing for jobs with millions of former slaves.

**The Emancipation Proclamation.** Despite his support for gradual emancipation, Lincoln soon realized that immediate action was necessary, both on military and moral grounds. Slaves were an asset to the Confederate war effort, and public opinion in the North was shifting in favor of emancipation. Following the Union "victory" at Antietam, the president issued his Preliminary Emancipation Proclamation (September 22, 1862), which granted freedom to all slaves in the Confederate states and in other areas of active rebellion as of January 1, 1863. The proclamation did not apply to the slaveholding border states, nor would it apply to any Confederate states that rejoined the Union before the deadline. The formal Emancipation Proclamation of January 1, 1863, specifically delineated the Confederate territory where slaves were freed, urged the slaves not to resort to violence except in self-defense, and confirmed that African Americans could serve in the Union army and navy.

Despite its limited scope, the Emancipation Proclamation redefined the purpose of the war. Southerners as well as northern Copperheads recognized this fact, and they condemned Lincoln's actions as tantamount to promoting a slave insurrection throughout the Confederacy. The slaves themselves responded with jubilation, not rebellion, and those who could fled to the Union lines, where their symbolic freedom could become a reality.

**Blacks in the Civil War.** Almost two hundred thousand African Americans fought in the Civil War, the majority of them former slaves. Organized into segregated units under white officers, they received less pay than white soldiers until Congress remedied the inequity in June 1864. At first, black troops were used only for menial jobs behind the lines. When finally allowed into combat, they distinguished themselves and earned grudging respect for their courage under fire. Black soldiers knew quite well that they faced summary execution or reenslavement if captured. Around thirty-seven thousand were killed during the war, a number that represents a significantly higher casualty rate than that of white soldiers.

The Confederacy used slaves as laborers to construct trenches and earthworks and as cooks and teamsters in military camps. With the South's manpower reserves dwindling in late 1864, Jefferson Davis proposed putting slaves into the army. The idea of slaves defending a government committed to the preservation of slavery while the opposing side was pledged to end it was one of the great ironies of the war. The Confederate Congress in fact passed legislation in March 1865 for the call-up of three hundred thousand slaves for the army, but the fighting stopped before the law went into effect.

## The Politics and Economics of the War

In the North, the Republican-controlled Congress implemented the party's domestic program. The **Pacific Railroad Act** (1862) authorized the construction of the first transcontinental line from both Omaha, Nebraska, and Sacramento, California. The Union Pacific and Central Pacific Railroad companies received more than sixty million acres of land at no cost and $20 million in very generous loans from the federal government, and together they completed the line in 1869. Republicans had always favored a liberal land policy, and the **Homestead Act** (1862) granted 160 acres free of charge (except for a small registration fee) to any farmer who worked the land for five years. The **Morrill Land Grant Act** (1862) was a boost to higher education in the country. States were given public lands for the purpose of establishing colleges for "agriculture and the mechanical arts." Today's state university systems are based on these "land grant" colleges.

**Financing the war.** The war was expensive for both sides. The Union raised money through higher tariffs, an excise tax that raised prices on most goods and services, and the imposition of the first federal income tax. The Bureau of Internal Revenue was established to collect taxes. Congress ordered paper money, known as **greenbacks,** to be printed as legal tender that could be used to pay debts but could not be redeemed for hard currency. Greenbacks and bonds issued by the federal government provided the main sources of revenue for the war effort. Bonds were sold through a network of agents and increased the national debt to almost $3 billion by 1865.

War created the opportunity for profiteering. The Union awarded millions of dollars in contracts to businesses for firearms, uniforms, and a broad range of military equipment and supplies. The contractors often took advantage of the federal government's largesse. One of the most notorious examples was manufacturers' use of **shoddy,** a cheap cloth made from compressed rag fiber, for making uniforms, which quickly fell apart. The word "shoddy" entered the English language as an adjective for anything of very poor quality.

The Confederacy, which was unable to secure the loans it expected from overseas, faced far worse financial problems than the Union. While taxes were raised in the same manner as in the North, they were difficult to collect and provided less than five percent of the South's wartime revenue. Confederate paper money was not declared legal tender, so there was little to no public confidence in it. Inflation became a major problem as more and more paper money was put into circulation; the value of a Confederate dollar dropped to just over one and a half cents in gold by the end of the war. Prices in the South rose by more than nine thousand percent between 1861 and 1865.

**Civil liberties and the war.** Some basic civil liberties were also casualties of the war. Lincoln, with the ultimate approval of Congress, suspended the writ of habeas corpus early in the conflict, and individuals suspected of disloyalty or active work against the Union were arrested without formal charges. While most of the nearly fourteen thousand who were detained were never brought to trial, those who were tried came under the jurisdiction of military courts. The reliance on military courts for trying civilians was declared unconstitutional by the Supreme Court in *Ex parte Milligan* in 1866.

## The Triumph of the Union

Despite his victories at Fredericksburg and Chancellorsville, General Lee realized that the Confederacy's only hope of victory was to bring the war to the North. In June 1863, the Army of Northern Virginia moved into Pennsylvania and confronted the Union forces at Gettysburg on July 1. The three-day battle ended in the South's worst defeat. Half of the fifteen thousand men under the command of General George Pickett, who charged the entrenched Union positions, were either killed, wounded, or captured. Lee had little choice but to retreat. At the same time, the Confederate troops under siege at Vicksburg surrendered and gave the Union complete control of the Mississippi River. The two engagements were the key turning points of the war; the Confederacy was effectively split and its armies never penetrated the North again.

**Grant in command.** In March 1864, following his victories in the West and his taking of Chattanooga (November 1863), Ulysses S. Grant was appointed commander of all Union forces. Lincoln had finally found his general after three years of war. The two main theaters of operation in 1864 were Virginia and Georgia. Grant fought a war of attrition, constantly attacking, regardless of the cost. Against Lee in the battles of the Wilderness, Spotsylvania Court House, and Cold Harbor and during the siege of Petersburg, the Union forces suffered extremely heavy casualties, but they continued to drive Lee's army deeper into Virginia.

In May, Grant ordered General William T. Sherman from Tennessee into Georgia. Union troops occupied Atlanta on September 1 and staged their infamous "March to the Sea" in the late fall. Sherman had all possible war materiel in Atlanta confiscated or destroyed, and he set fire to a large part of the city in the process. As his army moved through the state, crops were burned, livestock killed, and plantations and factories destroyed. Sherman's campaign of "total war" continued after he took Savannah in December and moved north into South Carolina.

**The election of 1864.** Despite a challenge from the Radical Republicans, the president was easily nominated for a second term with Andrew Johnson of Tennessee, a Unionist War Democrat, as his running mate. The platform called for the Confederacy's unconditional surrender and a constitutional amendment abolishing slavery. The Democrats chose General George McClellan as their candidate on an extreme peace platform that urged an immediate armistice, attacked Lincoln's handling of the war, and criticized emancipation. Public support for the war was uncertain as casualties mounted in 1864, but the president's campaign received a boost from Farragut's victory in Mobile (August 1864) and the fall of Atlanta. Lincoln won reelection with fifty-five percent of the vote and an overwhelming majority in the Electoral College. Most of the states allowed soldiers to vote in the field, and eighty percent of them cast their ballots for Lincoln.

**The end of the Confederacy.** With about half the number of troops as the Army of the Potomac, Lee was unable to break the siege at Petersburg. He broke off the engagement and tried to swing west and south to link up with what was left of his troops in North Carolina under General Johnston. Jefferson Davis abandoned Richmond and was eventually captured in Georgia in May. With the Confederate capital in Union hands, Lee found himself penned in by Grant's troops and those of General Philip Sheridan, and he asked for surrender terms on April 7, 1865. The formal surrender took place two days later in the town of Appomattox Court House. In the meantime, Sherman's army was moving into North Carolina to confront Johnston. Although Davis urged the general to fight on, Johnston surrendered his thirty-seven thousand men on April 26. By the end of May, all Confederate resistance throughout the South had come to an end. President Lincoln did not live to see the end of the war. He was assassinated by the actor John Wilkes Booth while watching a play in Washington's Ford's Theater on April 14, 1865.

Between 1861 and 1865, nearly three million men served in the Union and Confederate armies; more than 600,000 were killed, and an additional 275,000 were seriously wounded. Civil War casualties were almost as many as the combined losses in all other American wars through the Vietnam War. Although the fighting ended in the spring of 1865, the sectional divisions that led to the conflict continued to fester for generations. The immediate question was how the defeated states of the Confederacy would be treated. Although Lincoln had sounded a conciliatory note in his Second Inaugural Address a few days before his death, many others felt that the South must pay dearly for the war.

Well before the end of the Civil War, President Abraham Lincoln began formulating a plan to restore the Confederate states to the Union. His **Proclamation of Amnesty and Reconstruction** (December 1863) provided that if at least ten percent of a state's voters in the 1860 election accepted emancipation and took an oath of allegiance to the United States, then the state could form a new government and return to the Union. Blacks, who obviously had not voted in 1860, were excluded, as were most Confederate officials and army officers, who were disenfranchised unless they appealed for and received a presidential pardon. The Radical Republicans considered the "Ten Percent Plan" far too generous. The reconstruction approach they preferred was embodied in the **Wade-Davis bill** (July 1864), which called for the establishment of a military government in each state and required at least fifty percent of the eligible voters to swear allegiance to the United States. Only those who could take an "ironclad" oath that they had never willingly supported the Confederacy could vote or participate in the state constitutional conventions. Although Congress approved the Wade-Davis bill, Lincoln did not sign it before Congress adjourned, and the bill died (pocket veto).

## The Politics of Reconstruction

Following Lincoln's assassination, the task of implementing Reconstruction fell to his vice president, Andrew Johnson. A Democrat and the only senator from the South who remained loyal to the Union, Johnson at first seemed ready to take a hard line against the former Confederacy. He talked about punishing the traitors and breaking up the large plantations, but at the same time, he supported states' rights and had little sympathy for blacks. His policies after he became president were even more lenient than Lincoln's, and they caused a confrontation with the Radical Republicans in Congress that culminated in his impeachment.

**Johnson's policies.** In May 1865, with Congress out of session, Johnson began to implement his own Reconstruction program. Amnesty was granted to any southerner who took an oath of allegiance, with the exception of Confederate officials, officers, and wealthy landowners. Exclusion of the last group reflected Johnson's hatred of the planter aristocracy rather than some condition that had to do with restoring the former Confederate states. Those who were not eligible for amnesty could appeal for a pardon. Johnson appointed provisional governors and authorized them to set up state conventions, which in turn were charged with declaring secession illegal; repudiating Confederate debts; ratifying the **Thirteenth Amendment,** which abolished slavery in the United States; and scheduling elections. Once each convention's elections were held for governor, state legislators, and members of Congress, the states would be readmitted to the Union.

Several states refused to either repudiate the huge debt produced by the war or unconditionally accept the Thirteenth Amendment. Southern voters also elected to Congress high-ranking Confederate officials and officers, some of whom had not received one of the thirteen thousand pardons Johnson issued during the summer of 1865. The new state legislatures adopted so-called **black codes** to keep the newly freed African Americans, or **freedmen,** in their place. Blacks were required to either sign labor contracts or face arrest for vagrancy, and they were not allowed to serve on juries or testify in court. Despite these violations of both the letter and spirit of his program, the president announced that Reconstruction was complete in December 1865. However, Congress refused to seat the newly elected senators and representatives from the South.

**Johnson versus Congress.** Congress was divided among Radical, Moderate, and Conservative Republicans and Democrats. Rather than working with congressmen who might have supported his Reconstruction plan, Johnson alienated potential political allies by vetoing legislation intended to ensure civil rights for African Americans. A bill was introduced in February 1866 to reauthorize the one-year-old **Freedmen's Bureau** and allow it to try in military courts persons accused of depriving former slaves of their rights. Established in March

1865, the Bureau had provided blacks in the South with material assistance, schools, and guidance in settling on abandoned land. The new legislation was passed in July over Johnson's veto. The Civil Rights Act of 1866, which granted blacks born in the United States the same rights as white citizens, also became law (in April) over the president's objection.

Because of doubts about the constitutionality of the new Civil Rights Act, the congressional Joint Committee on Reconstruction drafted the **Fourteenth Amendment** to the Constitution. It was approved by both houses in June 1866. Essentially repudiating the 1857 *Dred Scott* decision, the amendment clearly states that "all persons born or naturalized in the United States … are citizens of the United States and of the State wherein they reside." It provides for due process and equal protection under the law. The amendment also denies to anyone who had participated in rebellion against the United States or had given aid and comfort to those in rebellion the right to hold any national or state office, an exclusion intended to undercut Johnson's pardon policy and protect the rights of blacks, particularly those of former slaves and particularly their right to vote.

Johnson denounced the Fourteenth Amendment and urged the southern states not to ratify it. Adoption of the amendment was an issue in the 1866 congressional elections, but the president's campaign against it did not work. Republicans were in control of both the House and Senate, and they gave a ringing endorsement to the amendment and congressional, not presidential, Reconstruction.

**Congressional Reconstruction.** The **First Reconstruction Act** (March 1867) invalidated the state governments established under Johnson's policies (except the government of Tennessee, which had ratified the Fourteenth Amendment) and divided the former Confederacy into five military districts. State conventions, elected by universal male suffrage, were to draw up new constitutions, which had to give blacks the right to vote and had to be approved by Congress. In fact, African Americans took part in all the conventions and made up the majority of delegates in South Carolina. Finally, each state legislature had to ratify the Fourteenth Amendment. The Reconstruction

Act was refined by subsequent legislation. In June 1868, Congress determined that Alabama, Arkansas, Florida, Georgia, Louisiana, North Carolina, and South Carolina had met the requirements, and the states were admitted to the Union. When duly elected black representatives were expelled from the Georgia legislature, Georgia once again fell under military rule. Georgia, along with Mississippi, Texas, and Virginia, had to satisfy an additional condition: ratification of the **Fifteenth Amendment,** which prohibited the states from denying a citizen the right to vote because of race, color, or previous condition of servitude. The four states did not rejoin the Union until 1870.

Women's rights advocates Susan B. Anthony and Elizabeth Cady Stanton were incensed that the Fifteenth Amendment did not also list gender among the conditions that could not be used to deny a citizen the right to vote. The long alliance between the women's movement and the abolitionist cause broke, and women struggled on their own for another half century for the right to vote.

Congress enacted its Reconstruction program over Johnson's veto. Determined to prevent Johnson from interfering with their plan, Radical Republicans pushed through two pieces of legislation in March 1867 intended to severely limit presidential power. The **Command of the Army Act** prevented the president from issuing orders to the military except through the general of the army, who at the time was Ulysses S. Grant; additionally, the commanding general could not be removed without the Senate's consent. The **Tenure of Office Act** required the president to obtain approval from the Senate to remove any officeholder that the Senate had confirmed. Johnson and Secretary of War Edwin Stanton were bitter enemies, and the president wanted to get rid of him. Stanton was suspended in August 1867 and replaced with Grant as an interim. This was all Congress needed to begin impeachment proceedings.

**The impeachment of Johnson.** Under the Constitution, the House of Representatives acts as a grand jury in impeachment cases and determines whether there is enough evidence to bring an official to trial. In February 1868, after months of investigation, the House voted to impeach the president, largely on the grounds that Johnson had violated the Tenure of Office Act in firing Edwin Stanton. It was left to the Senate to try the president—with Chief Justice Salmon P. Chase presiding—and determine whether he should be removed from office. Enough Republican senators appreciated the fact that Johnson's offenses were political and that they did not fall under the "high crimes and misdemeanors" specified in the Constitution for presidential impeachment. The vote in the Senate was thirty-five to nineteen in favor of conviction, one short of the necessary two-thirds majority.

## Reconstruction in Practice

Reconstruction brought important social changes to former slaves. Families that had been separated before and during the Civil War were reunited, and slave marriages were formalized through legally recognized ceremonies. Families also took advantage of the schools established by the Freedmen's Bureau and the expansion of public education, albeit segregated, under the Reconstruction legislatures. New opportunities for higher education also became available with the founding soon after the Civil War of black colleges, such as Howard University in Washington, D.C., and Fisk University in Nashville, Tennessee. The number of African-American churches grew significantly and became social and political centers as well as houses of worship. Black ministers assumed a leadership role in the community and were among the first elected officials. The most fundamental concern of blacks through all of the changes, though, was economic survival.

**African Americans in the southern economy.** Any hope of large-scale black property ownership disappeared soon after the Civil War. Although Congress considered breaking up plantations as part of Reconstruction, Radical Republicans were more interested in securing suffrage for and protecting the civil rights of African Americans than in reforming southern land distribution. The Southern Homestead Act of 1866 did provide 44 million acres to freedmen, but the land was marginal at best. Whites generally refused to sell land to former slaves, who, in any event, did not have the money to buy it or the farm implements needed to work it. The upshot for the large, poor, and landless black population was **sharecropping.** White landowners divided their plantations into thirty- to fifty-acre plots; blacks leased the land, worked it, and paid half of the crop to the owner.

Sharecroppers needed credit to buy seeds, tools, and other supplies. Under the **crop-lien system,** they put up the proceeds from the sale of their harvest as collateral. A poor harvest or a succession of bad years would plunge sharecroppers further into debt, leaving them unable to pay the merchant who had advanced the credit or make the in-kind payment to the landowner. The system kept sharecroppers in a cycle of perpetual poverty from which they were unable to escape.

**Politics in the South during Reconstruction.** Reconstruction meant that blacks in the South participated in the political process for the first time. In addition to taking part in the state conventions, African Americans served in the state legislatures and were elected to Congress. During Reconstruction, fourteen black representatives and two black senators served in Congress; however, no African American became a governor of a southern state, and only in South Carolina did the number of black officeholders reflect their voting strength. Those elected were the African-American elite: men who had been free before the Civil War, landowners, the educated, and clergy. The African-American voters helped keep Republicans in control of the former Confederacy, and they consistently went to the "party of Lincoln" in national elections well into the twentieth century.

Although Reconstruction brought about a revolution in black political power (short-lived though it was), African Americans did not have a voting majority throughout the South, so the Republicans needed white support as well. White Republicans, mainly yeoman farmers who had leaned toward the Union during the Civil War, were called **scalawags** by die-hard Confederates; these southern Republicans backed such federal programs as public education, road construction, and rebuilding the economy. Another political force during Reconstruction were the northerners who went South after the war in

search of lucrative government work—the so-called **carpetbaggers.**
The "coalition" between black Republicans, white Republicans, and
northerners was fragile indeed. Relying primarily on the race issue,
Democrats were able to regain control of state governments throughout the South during the 1870s.

**The rise of the Ku Klux Klan.** The Ku Klux Klan, formed in Tennessee in 1866, was one of several secret societies that used intimidation and force, including murder, to advance white supremacy and
bring an end to Republican rule. These organizations formed a tacit
alliance with the Democratic party in the South and played a key role
in bringing about **"Redemption,"** the Democrats' term for their re-
gaining control of the old Confederacy. Although the Klan was officially disbanded in 1869, Congress took action against its activities
in a series of laws known collectively as the **Enforcement Acts**
(1870–71). The legislation, which was intended to "enforce" the
Fourteenth and Fifteenth Amendments and make it a crime for anyone to interfere with a citizen's right to vote, included the **Ku Klux
Klan Act,** which outlawed conspiring, wearing disguises, and intimidating officials for the purpose of undermining the Constitution.
President Grant used the law to suspend the writ of habeas corpus in
parts of South Carolina, and he successfully prosecuted the Klan in
that state. In the long run, however, federal officials found it as difficult to root out the Klan and other white supremacist groups as it was
to make it possible for blacks to exercise their right to vote.

## The Grant Administration and the End of Reconstruction

As the Civil War retreated into history, issues other than Reconstruction began to dominate the political agenda. The Republican party
slowly backed away from programs and reforms that might have improved the quality of life for African Americans and protected their
rights, so recently made a part of the Constitution. A combination of
Supreme Court decisions and a lack of political will brought an end
to Reconstruction.

**The election of Grant.** Ulysses S. Grant was nominated as the Republican candidate for president in 1868. The man who accepted Lee's surrender at Appomattox Court House was expected to earn the veteran vote, while his lack of political experience meant he would likely follow the lead of Congress. The electorate had a clear choice. The Republican platform endorsed Reconstruction, supported paying off the national debt in gold, and defended black suffrage in the South; the Democrats condemned Reconstruction as tantamount to a military dictatorship, favored soft money (wanting to keep the millions of dollars in Civil War greenbacks in circulation), and hoped to win votes from whites who felt that blacks were benefiting too much from Reconstruction. Although Grant easily won the electoral vote over his relatively unknown Democratic challenger, Horatio Seymour, the popular vote was much closer than anticipated. Freedmen in the South, casting their ballots for the first time, provided Grant with the margin of victory.

**Foreign policy and domestic issues.** To its credit, the Grant administration settled the simmering dispute with Great Britain over the damages caused by British-built Confederate ships during the Civil War. Both countries agreed in 1871 to allow an international tribunal to resolve the so-called **Alabama claims,** named for the infamous Confederate raider. The tribunal ruled in favor of the United States, which was awarded more than $15 million.

After the purchase of Alaska from Russia in 1867, some government officials looked for other opportunities to expand beyond the continental United States. Although Congress had rejected buying the Virgin Islands, Grant looked toward the Caribbean again in 1870. His treaty to annex Santo Domingo (the Dominican Republic), however, did not even have the support of his cabinet, and the Senate refused to ratify it.

On the domestic side, Grant's first term was marred by scandals. The president's brother-in-law was involved with railroad magnates Jay Gould and Jim Fisk in a scheme to corner the gold market. On the evening of the 1872 election, Vice President Schuyler Colfax was implicated in the activities of the Crédit Mobilier, a construction company that skimmed profits from the Union Pacific Railroad. Corruption at local levels gained national attention at the same time. William

Marcy Tweed, the political boss of New York City, and a group of associates known as the **Tweed Ring** purloined millions from the municipal coffers through kickbacks from city contractors and billing for work never done.

The weaknesses in Grant's leadership and concern over the future of Reconstruction caused a split in the Republican party. Liberal Republicans held a separate convention in 1872 and nominated for president newspaper editor Horace Greeley, who was also the standard-bearer of the Democratic party. Greeley, who had strongly favored full emancipation during the war, supported an immediate end to Reconstruction during his campaign. The Liberal Republicans also advocated civil service reform and an end to the granting of public land to railroads. Despite all the problems in his administration, Grant was reelected by even wider margins in the electoral and popular votes than in 1868.

**The panic of 1873.** During his second term, Grant was still unable to curb the graft in his administration. Secretary of War William Belknap was impeached by the House, and he resigned in disgrace for taking bribes from dishonest Indian agents. The president's personal secretary was involved with the **Whiskey Ring,** a group of distillers who evaded paying internal revenue taxes. A much more pressing concern though was the state of the economy.

In 1873, overspeculation in railroad stocks led to a major economic panic. The failure of Jay Cooke's investment bank was followed by the collapse of the stock market and the bankruptcy of thousands of businesses; crop prices plummeted and unemployment soared. Much of the problem was related to the use of greenbacks for currency. Hard-money advocates insisted that paper money had to be backed by gold to curb inflation and level price fluctuations, but farmers and manufacturers, who needed easy credit, wanted even more greenbacks put in circulation, a policy that Grant ultimately opposed. He recommended and the Congress enacted legislation in 1875 providing for the redemption of greenbacks in gold. Because the Treasury needed time to build up its gold reserves, redemption did not go into effect for another four years, by which time the longest depression in American history had come to an end.

**The end of Reconstruction.** In 1872, Congress passed the **General Amnesty Act,** which removed all restrictions against former Confederate officials. The Supreme Court narrowly interpreted the Fourteenth Amendment in the *Slaughterhouse* **cases** in 1873. In a 5–4 decision, the Court held that the amendment's rights applied only to a person's citizenship in the United States, not to citizenship in the states; the federal government had little recourse when state law violated the civil rights of individuals.

Congress prohibited discrimination based on race in public places and guaranteed the right of blacks to serve on juries through the **Civil Rights Act of 1875.** The legislation—really the last hurrah for the Radical Republicans—was not enforced, however. By 1876, both political parties were ready to abandon Reconstruction and its legacy, and in 1883, the eight-year-old Civil Rights Act was declared unconstitutional by the Supreme Court.

**The election of 1876.** In 1876, the Republicans looked for a presidential candidate untouched by the scandals of the Grant administration and chose Ohio governor Rutherford B. Hayes, a man with a well-deserved reputation for honesty. Samuel J. Tilden, the crusading governor of New York, who had taken on the Tweed Ring and the political bosses in his state, was the Democratic nominee. There was little difference between the two men. Both supported hard money, both promised reforms in the way government did business, and both were considered moderates on Reconstruction. The election turned out to be the most controversial in American history.

Although earning three hundred thousand more popular votes than Hayes, Tilden won just 184 electoral votes, one short of the majority needed for election. Twenty electoral votes from Florida, Louisiana, Oregon, and South Carolina were in dispute, as both sides traded charges of ballot fraud. The Constitution offered no guidance on how to resolve the matter. In January 1877, Congress appointed a special commission made up of seven Republicans, seven Democrats, and one independent to investigate the contested electoral votes. When the independent, Supreme Court Justice David Davis, resigned, he was replaced by a Republican. Not surprisingly, the commission voted a consistent 8–7 in favor of Hayes.

Congress was ready to declare Hayes the winner of the election, but the Democrat-controlled House of Representatives threatened a filibuster that would delay final action. In return for an end to Reconstruction, the southern Democrats would abandon Tilden. The **Compromise of 1877** made Hayes president in return for a Republican pledge to remove federal troops from Louisiana and South Carolina, an action that would bring to a close the last vestige of military occupation of the South. The Democrats also wanted a southerner appointed to Hayes's cabinet and money for internal improvements, specifically a subsidy for a transcontinental railroad along a southern route through Texas. Hayes made David Key of Tennessee postmaster general, then a cabinet post that was a rich source of patronage. For their part, congressional southerners agreed to support the civil-rights constitutional amendments.

With the end of Reconstruction, the Republicans effectively abandoned southern blacks. The years ahead saw segregation institutionalized and the civil rights of African Americans sharply curtailed by state law, particularly the right to vote. Politically, the Democrats controlled what became known as the "solid South," until the federal government once again committed itself to protect all citizens, regardless of race.